THE SONG WRITER'S MARKET GUIDE TO SONG & DEMO SUBMISSION FORMATS

FROM THE EDITORS OF SONGWRITER'S MARKET

WRITER'S DIGEST BOOKS

CINCINNATI, OHIO

The Songwriter's Market Guide to Song and Demo Submission Formats. Copyright © 1994 by *Songwriter's Market*. Printed and bound in the United States of America. All rights reserved. No part of this book may be reproduced in any form or by any electronic or mechanical means including information storage and retrieval systems without permission in writing from the publisher, except by a reviewer, who may quote brief passages in a review. Published by Writer's Digest Books, an imprint of F&W Publications, Inc., 1507 Dana Avenue, Cincinnati, Ohio 45207. 1-800-289-0963. First edition.

This hardcover edition of *The Songwriter's Market Guide to Song and Demo Submission Formats* features a "self-jacket" that eliminates the need for a separate dust jacket. It provides sturdy protection for your book while it saves paper, trees and energy.

98 97 96 95 94   5 4 3 2 1

Library of Congress Cataloging-in-Publication Data

    The Songwriter's market guide to song and demo submission formats / by the editors of Songwriter's market.
      p.   cm.
   Includes index.
   ISBN 0-89879-544-3
   1. Music trade—Vocational guidance. 2. Popular music—Writing and publishing. I. Songwriter's market.
ML3790.S68 1994
782.42'023'73—dc20   93-44930
                                               CIP
                                             MN

Edited by Donna Collingwood, assisted by Cindy Laufenberg, Argie Manolis and Mark Garvey
Designed by Clare Finney
Cover designed by Magno Relojo, Jr.

The following page constitutes an extension of this copyright page.

PERMISSIONS

CONTENTS

INTRODUCTION

Songwriters, like writers and visual artists, must create good first impressions. When submitting your original work to a music publisher, record company manager or play production house, that first impression is often in the form of a submission package.

We, the editors of *Songwriter's Market*, have sought out the advice of industry professionals about making first impressions with professional submissions, and we have compiled that advice in an easy-access format. You'll find chapters that offer advice for submitting to music publishers, record companies, record producers, managers and agents, commercial music firms, play producers, fine arts organizations and contests. Each chapter discusses how to approach each segment of the music industry, what constitutes a "demo" or "press kit" in that segment, and how to get your foot in the door. Following the instruction are visual guides for compiling a professional package.

For example, if you want to submit a score for a play, turn to chapter nine and you'll find instruction from the co-directors of Broadway on Sunset. You'll also find a sample query letter, submission letter, bio, synopsis, cover page, cassette label and more.

Some chapters present sample bios, some present sample cover letters, some include sample telephone scripts and others, business cards. If you're submitting to an agent, read chapter four, of course, but look at some of the samples in other chapters also. Naturally, everyone will want to read the chapters on copyright and record-keeping—music business essentials.

An insider's view of the process, however, is not a guarantee of success. In this competitive business, you must give yourself every advantage, and a sloppy cover letter or unattractive bio can almost guarantee rejection.

This book brings together, in one place, quick guidelines to the last-minute submission details that could make or break your chance to sell your material. We hope you'll refer to it often.

CHAPTER 1

DEMO FORMATS AND PACKAGING

ince the 1970s, cassette tapes have been the music industry standard for submissions. Not only do most executives have cassette decks in their cars and homes, but they also have them in their offices. Some may have a personal cassette player to listen to on the run. The convenience of cassette tapes and the accessibility of playback decks overcome any sonic limitations of the form.

Before rock music, reel to reel tape was the norm for submissions, as were acetates, vinyl versions of songs and low-budget records in a test format. These were commonly made by music publishers to play for artists and record companies. Even though digital audio tape (DAT) is beginning to make some inroads, it's safe to say that it will probably never be as accessible as cassette tape. The latest technological wrinkle is the digital cassette tape, which is being developed in Japan and will probably be available in the United States shortly.

ABOUT CASSETTE TAPES

Although new technologies are developing constantly, cassette tapes are here to stay. They are conveniently sized and can be reproduced inexpensively via built-in microphones. They are affordable by virtually every segment of our society. Because of this, a huge number of cassette tapes are purchased each year. Even though this format is losing ground to the CD, the cassette remains the people's medium.

Most cassette decks will accept three formulations of cassette tape: normal bias, chrome or high position tape, and metal tape. Although many prerecorded tapes are still generated in the normal range for cassette duplication, it is recommended that you use chrome, or high position tape. These tapes sound good and actually play back with more of the high frequencies than are recorded onto them. The downside to this sonic excitement is the noise generated by more high frequencies. In most forms of popular music, however, this is not a problem. Metal tape, made from chromium dioxide metal particles, is capable of recording and playing back at higher decibel levels than chrome or normal tape, but again, a significant amount of noise is generated. Normal tape is the cheapest, metal the most expensive, and high position or chrome is in the middle.

No industry professional would ever consider submitting songs on a commercial tape that can be purchased from the local stereo store, no matter what the grade or manufacturer. For making multiple copies of songs on tape as a part of a publishing demo or an artist package, it's necessary to give a good first impression. Fortunately, it's possible to create a good-looking and professional package by following a few strategic guidelines.

Cassette tapes can be purchased in bulk from a reputable company that specializes in custom length tapes. This is the cheapest way to purchase tapes. These companies acquire enormous industrial reels of tape and subdivide it into the exact configuration you need (i.e. five minutes, ten minutes, twenty minutes, etc.), then load the tapes into the shells and ship or sell them to you. Note: It is best if your submissions fit on only one side of a cassette tape. The tape should be no longer than thirty minutes. Longer tapes are actually thinner, with a proportionate loss of quality.

About Duplication

When duplicating cassette tapes you have a choice of two methods. One method: Your master tape is played on a master playback machine that feeds the signal to ten or more slave cassette machines simultaneously. This process is repeated until the requisite number of tapes are made. The cassette recorders should record at so-called normal speed for this process. High speed is common for spoken word tapes but should never be used for music.

Although this process is very common, it has some distinct disadvantages. Identical decks have individual characteristics, and ten tape decks can have ten sets of quirks in their sounds as well as differing frequency responses. Since it's not feasible for you to listen to every single tape you send, quality control is virtually impossible.

When duplicating a number of tapes, have the facility make test copies. After paying the facility, take the tapes home and listen to them repeatedly: in the car, in your home studio, wherever you're used to listening to music. Compare these copies to the reference tape that you (hopefully) had made at the studio where you recorded. Make sure that the copies sound as good as the reference tape. Keep in mind that most top of the line recording studios have five or more sets of playback speakers, ranging from tiny little Aurotones to monster JBL earth-shaking cabinets. Beware the big, bad speakers, since they can certainly cloud your perceptions of the music by sheer force of kinesthetic thunder.

Often your master tape, even a DAT, will need equalization to make the tape copy come out right. The importance of taking your time with this can't be overemphasized. If your duplicating facility balks at allowing you to take your time and listen thoroughly, go elsewhere immediately! Watch for tape speed discrepancies also, since cassette decks typically run at faster or slower speeds depending on their age, make, and wear and tear.

The other method of duplicating cassettes is by making what is known as a bin loop master tape on ½" recording tape or a comparable professional format from your master tape. The bin loop master has tones at the beginning and the end of the musical information that are used to tell the duplicating machines when to begin and end recording. A pancake of cassette tape (generally in a 5,000- to 10,000-foot length) is then loaded into a special duplicating machine. The tape is recorded and loaded into cassette shells with only the exact length of tape necessary in each shell.

The advantages to duplicating this way are many. Since there is only one recording machine, the inherent problems of different machines and quality control are eliminated. Also, cassette tapes recorded in the shell will have a certain amount of variable wow and flutter, since the cassette itself is basically a cheap object, and much better used in a playback rather than a record mode. By recording with a bin loop master, a high quality of sound can consistently be achieved. Note: Even if you have to pay for set up of the bin loop master, have test cassettes made first. Duplicating and reduplicating tape copies until the proper sound is achieved is frustrating, time consuming and expensive.

Always ask for reference cassettes of anything you wish to have duplicated. Take them home and listen to them repeatedly. Be a stickler, and above all, trust your instincts—because it's your music.

About Shell-on Printing

In recent years, clear plastic cassette shells have become popular. These shells were first developed by the Shape Company, which designed them with an azimuth bridge piece that held the tape in place to control tape movement that could adversely affect sound. These shells have been endlessly replicated by other companies without the bridge piece, but in the same plastic configuration, usually with a graphite piece inside. The clear shells are very attractive with shell-on printing: Song titles and other information are duplicated directly on the cassette shell. In this process, a mechanical plate of the appropriate information is made. The information is then transferred via a stamping mechanism. The set up for this process alone can add at least $35 to your budget. But if you are creating a product for sale, for an artist package, or if you have a generous budget (and high aspirations), you may wish to investigate the possibility of shell-on printing.

Labels

Printing facilities can create a duplicate cassette label (see sample, page 7) from your camera-ready master for a very low price. Commercially generated labels can be duplicated in bulk and come in a variety of colors. Unless your band is on the outer fringes, use a simply colored label—white, beige, light grey, etc. Make sure that any information on your tape is easy to read (it will be with the aforementioned colors), and beware the dreaded slippery labels to which nothing will adhere, especially typewriter letters. Use easy-to-read print styles, such as Times or Helvetica, for information.

Always include this information on your label:

1. Song title(s)
2. Songwriter name(s)
3. Artist name (if an artist package)
4. Copyright date (e.g., ©1992)
5. A contact telephone number

ABOUT J-CARDS

Other information such as length of songs, pertinent publishing information and performing rights affiliation (if applicable) should be on the J-cards, or cassette box inserts. J-cards (see sample, page 8) are named for their distinctive shape, which resembles the letter *J* when folded to fit into the cassette box. The cards are made from cardboard (though not too stiff, they need to fold neatly) and printed on both sides, front and back, plus the spine. Many record companies add more foldout panels to their releases for lyrics, but for our purposes we'll examine the single, two-sided J-card. The front cover should be a picture of the artist or cover artwork for an artist submission package. Always keep in mind that this is a small-scale format, and that simple uncluttered photos and art are preferable.

To properly duplicate J-cards, you'll need camera-ready art. If using a photo, it will have to be screened for duplication. Screening is a process by which photos are prepared for mass duplication by creating a dot image of the photo. A typesetter, lithographer or stat house can help you create the dot image from either a positive or a negative image, and a typesetter can help to set the type to construct the J-card. If you have access to a computer and laser printer, you can even do it yourself. Keep in mind that your master must be the exact size for duplication.

Include this information on your J-card:

1. Song title(s)
2. Songwriter name(s)
3. Publishing information (if applicable)

4. Performing rights affiliation (if applicable)
5. Studio and engineer names (artist demos)
6. Producer name (artist demos)
7. Musician names (artist demos)
8. Contact phone number

Don't Thank Everyone: Not Yet!

You may have seen cassette J-cards with panel upon panel of acknowledgements and thank-yous. For a demo, this is presumptuous and pretentious. Save it for your album. But never forget to include songwriter names; it seems astounding, but many record companies exclude this information on their releases, despite education and lobbying from songwriter organizations. For artist demos and submissions, acknowledging musicians is only proper. But if you or your producer have used sequencing or sampling, it's not necessary to include this information, particularly if it sounds real! Some artists make up names for fictitious musicians to give the impression that more people are involved in the project.

ABOUT O-CARDS

O-cards are simply four-sided sleeves that completely surround the cassette tapes. They have information printed on the front and back and are then shrink-wrapped. If you've seen cassette singles for sale in your local retail outlet, these are generally packaged with O-cards. These cards are printed in a flat format. One side of the card is then glued, creating the *O* effect. The advantage to this format is that no tape box is used, saving money in preparing the tapes. Tapes with O-cards are suitable for sale at gigs or retail stores. One disadvantage in using the shrink-wrapped, O-card format for presentation and submissions to music industry people is that it takes time to remove shrink-wrap, and, believe it or not, this simple effort may keep your tape from being played. Unless you are in the business of merchandising tapes, it's better to stick to the cassette-box format.

ABOUT TAPE BOXES

The plastic cassette boxes are referred to as Norelco boxes after their manufacturer. Even though they have been duplicated, all boxes of this type share identical characteristics: They are easily smudged, scratched, dropped and broken, but are relatively cheap in bulk and allow the contents, your tape and J-card, to be clearly seen. The soft plastic boxes that are hinged on the end are opaque, so their contents aren't as visible. They're not as effective in making presentations when pictures and graphics are important. However, they do retain their shape well, so for submissions to a publisher they are actually preferable. These cheaper boxes will help keep overall costs down if you send out a lot of submissions.

CONCLUSION

Coordination of all elements of your presentation is the true mark of professionalism. Integration of your image, sound, tape and J-card should give you the best possible shot at getting noticed. You can get many good ideas by examining the commercial products in your local record store. The presentation of your music won't make it any better; ultimately, it is your music that will sell your act. Still, a professional presentation will most likely guarantee your music at least a listen.

SAMPLE LABEL

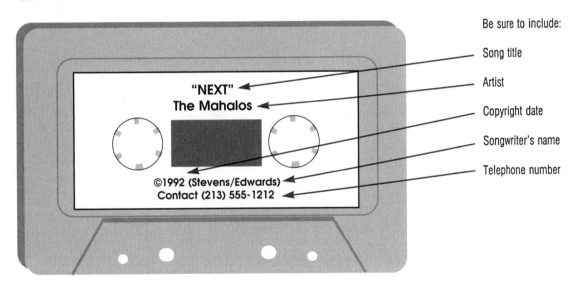

Be sure to include:

Song title

Artist

Copyright date

Songwriter's name

Telephone number

SAMPLE J-CARD

Always include:

Song titles

Songwriter

Publishing information

Performing rights affiliation

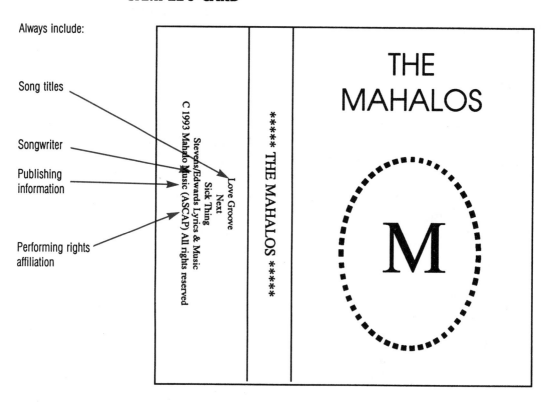

Producer

Engineer

Executive producer

Musicians

Studio

Manager (with telephone number)

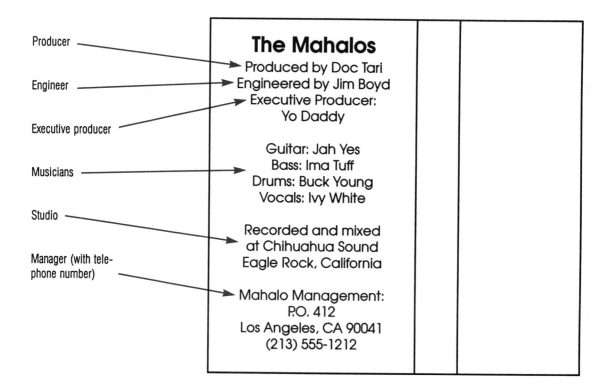

The Mahalos
Produced by Doc Tari
Engineered by Jim Boyd
Executive Producer:
Yo Daddy

Guitar: Jah Yes
Bass: Ima Tuff
Drums: Buck Young
Vocals: Ivy White

Recorded and mixed
at Chihuahua Sound
Eagle Rock, California

Mahalo Management:
P.O. 412
Los Angeles, CA 90041
(213) 555-1212

CHAPTER 2

LYRIC AND LEAD SHEETS

L yric and lead sheets can add to your submission package in certain cases. Look through the various chapters to see when use of a lyric sheet is recommended. This chapter will help you decide when to include them and how to prepare them.

LYRIC SHEETS

A lyric sheet—a sheet of paper containing the typed lyrics to a song—is a necessary item in any song submission. The purpose of the lyric sheet is to make the lyrics of your song, which are easily misheard, totally accessible to the professional listener, most of whom prefer to have a lyric sheet to consult either while or after listening to the song.

Less Is More

To make sure your lyrics are presented as clearly as possible on a lyric sheet, keep in mind that less is more. Besides the lyrics themselves, the only information the lyric sheet needs to contain is the copyright notice and your name, address and phone number.

In their eagerness to communicate, many songwriters tend to put too much information on their lyric sheets. Some insert chord changes over the lyrics, some write in the melody note names, some label all the sections of the song until there are more labels than lyrics. If you must label a song section, the chorus is your best choice. Never send a handwritten lyric sheet or a typed lyric sheet with handwritten chord notations.

Paper

Using letterhead paper gives a more professional look to the lyric sheet, but lyrics typed on plain twenty-pound bond 8½″ × 11″ paper are acceptable. Sending out lots of lyric sheets on original letterhead stationery can be expensive.

An economical way to make good-looking lyric sheets is to temporarily tape the letterhead portion from a piece of stationery on the top of a plain sheet and make copies of the composite. On a good copying machine, the line between the two pieces of paper will not reproduce.

White paper is always acceptable, but using paper of a different color can break the monotony for the professional listener and help distinguish your work. One songwriter uses purple paper and envelopes and her easily recognizable tape submissions and correspondence have earned her the sobriquet, "The Purple Lady." By choosing a signature color, she has the advantage of being not just another white envelope on the pile. To color coordinate your lyric sheets with your previously printed letterhead, type the lyrics on white paper and then copy them onto colored paper. If your original is on colored paper, however, you risk poor-quality copies.

Format

There is no carved-in-stone format for lyric sheets, but the sample lyric sheet on page 13 contains the essential elements you need as they would appear on letterhead stationery. The idea is to make the lyric sheet as clean and uncluttered as possible. Spacing guidelines are given with the ultimate aim of having the lyric centered from top to bottom on the space available. In other words, when you're finished, the lyric should not be squeezed up at the top of the page or running off the page. If your lyric sheet is typed on plain paper, your name, address and phone number (including area code) should be typed at the bottom of the page, at least two spaces below the copyright notice.

LEAD SHEETS

Lead sheets communicate the melody, chords and lyrics of a song in written form. Before the new copyright law came into effect in 1978, songwriters were required to submit a lead sheet with every song sent to the United States Copyright Office for registration. Now, since a cassette recording and lyric sheet are sufficient documentation for copyright registration, lead sheets are no longer needed or required as part of the copyright process.

When to Send a Lead Sheet

It is not appropriate to send a lead sheet with most song submission packages. In fact, including a lead sheet with your popular song demo will probably evoke a negative reaction in the professional listener because it conveys the message that your are not hip to what's happening in the music business. The easier it is to handle your song submission, the better the listener will feel about it. Therefore include only the essentials.

A lead sheet can be helpful in the demo-making process, especially if you

SAMPLE LYRIC SHEET

(Your logo here)

W&T Music Publishing
1234 Our Street
Hollywood, CA 90028
213-463-7178

Leave at least ½" of space between letter-head information and title

I LOVE A GOOD LYRIC
by Willie Words and Tania Tunes

Center the title, capi-talize or make the type a larger point size

Center the writers' names under the title

Capitalize the first word in each line
Start off your lyric flush with the left margin
Each line corresponds with a melodic phrase
Since this is the verse, we won't label the section

Start the lyric two to four spaces down

Skip a line between sections, and these two lines, of course
Are sometimes called lift and sometimes pre-chorus

Indent chorus and capitalize title

CHORUS:
    I LOVE A GOOD LYRIC
    And I want to show it
    I LOVE A GOOD LYRIC
    And I'll let you know it
    By keeping it simple
    And keeping it clean
    I LOVE A GOOD LYRIC—sheet, I mean

Lift repeat can be writ-ten out in full

Don't retype Chorus lyrics

We're back to the verse and the verse format
Don't worry too much about punctuation
You can't sing a comma or even a dash
All you need is the lyrical information

Two returns

Skip a line between sections, and these two lines, of course
Are sometimes called lift and sometimes pre-chorus

CHORUS: (Repeat)

© 1992 W&T Music Publishing
(Type your address and phone number here—if not using letterhead.)

Copyright notice must include © symbol, the year the song was written and the name of the copyright owner. In this case, we are using the name of the songwriters' pub-lishing company. If you do not have a pub-lishing company name, use your own name

SAMPLE CHORD SHEET

Clef not necessary. Indicate key and time signatures in first measure only, unless they change during song

Always put writer's credits below and to the right of the title

Indicate rhythm by strokes

Indicate chord changes on the beat where they occur

Label large song sections such as "Verse," "Lift" and "Chorus"

Place lyric directly under where it occurs in the music

Chord name on top, bass note on bottom

Always include copyright notice on all written and taped copies of songs

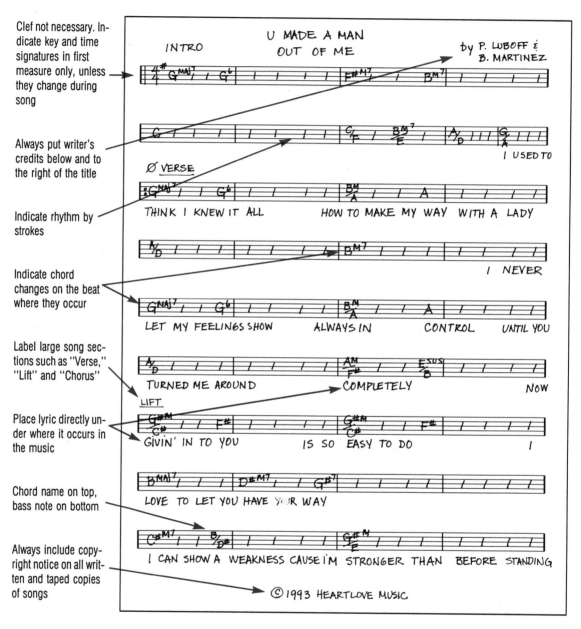

Courtesy of Heartlove Music, 1993

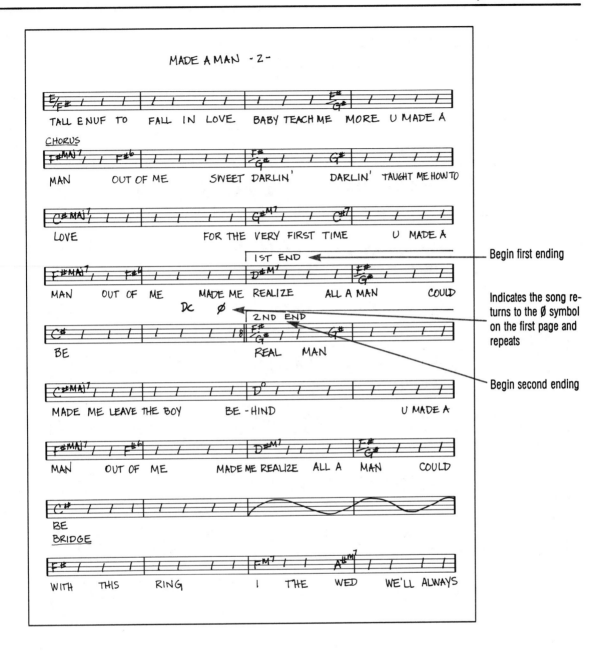

MADE A MAN - 2 -

E/F# / / / / / / / / F#/G# / / / /
TALL ENUF TO FALL IN LOVE BABY TEACH ME MORE U MADE A

CHORUS
F#MAJ7 / / F#6 / / / / / F#/G# / / / G# / / / /
MAN OUT OF ME SWEET DARLIN' DARLIN' TAUGHT ME HOW TO

C#MAJ7 / / / / / / G#M7 / / / C#7 / / / /
LOVE FOR THE VERY FIRST TIME U MADE A

1ST END ← Begin first ending
F#MAJ7 / / F#6 / / / / D#M7 / / / F#/G# / / /
MAN OUT OF ME MADE ME REALIZE ALL A MAN COULD

Dc ⌀ ← Indicates the song returns to the Ø symbol on the first page and repeats
2ND END
C# / / / / / / / F#/G# / / G# / / / /
BE REAL MAN
↑ Begin second ending

C#MAJ7 / / / / / / D° / / / / / / /
MADE ME LEAVE THE BOY BE-HIND U MADE A

F#MAJ7 / / F#6 / / / / D#M7 / / F#/G# / / /
MAN OUT OF ME MADE ME REALIZE ALL A MAN COULD

C# / / / / / / /
BE

BRIDGE
F# / / / / / / / F#M7 / / A#M7 / / / /
WITH THIS RING I THE WED WE'LL ALWAYS

SAMPLE HANDWRITTEN LEAD SHEET

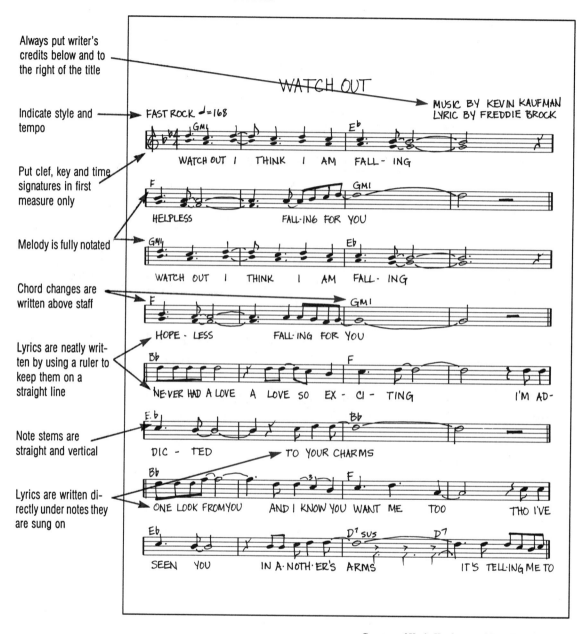

Always put writer's credits below and to the right of the title

Indicate style and tempo

Put clef, key and time signatures in first measure only

Melody is fully notated

Chord changes are written above staff

Lyrics are neatly written by using a ruler to keep them on a straight line

Note stems are straight and vertical

Lyrics are written directly under notes they are sung on

WATCH OUT

MUSIC BY KEVIN KAUFMAN
LYRIC BY FREDDIE BROCK

FAST ROCK ♩=168

WATCH OUT I THINK I AM FALL - ING

HELPLESS   FALL-ING FOR YOU

WATCH OUT I THINK I AM FALL-ING

HOPE - LESS   FALL-ING FOR YOU

NE-VER HAD A LOVE   A LOVE SO EX - CI - TING   I'M AD-

DIC - TED   TO YOUR CHARMS

ONE LOOK FROM YOU   AND I KNOW YOU WANT ME   TOO   THO I'VE

SEEN   YOU   IN A-NOTH-ER'S ARMS   IT'S TELL-ING ME TO

Courtesy of Kevin Kaufman and Freddie Brock, 1984

SAMPLE COMPUTER-GENERATED LEAD SHEET

Christmas Dreams

Words & Music by Gene Megs, B.M.I.

The laser-printed lead sheet has a polished, professional, finished-product look. MIDI (Musical Instrument Digital Interface) software can print out exactly what you play and record. If you have the proper hardware and software, you can easily produce this kind of lead sheet

If you don't have your own set-up, there are services that will transcribe from your tape or input from your handwritten lead sheet

Courtesy of Gene Megs and Megaphone Music, 1991

CHAPTER 3

COPYRIGHT

Any book about submission formats would be incomplete without a chapter on copyright. Copyright laws are perhaps the most confusing part of the business of songwriting. To protect themselves, all songwriters and artists should have a basic understanding of the laws and the copyright registration process. To make it easier to use this chapter, the information has been arranged in question and answer format.

Q: What does the copyright law allow you to do as a songwriter?
A: The copyright law provides the following protections: the right to make and sell copies of your original song anywhere in the world in the form of sheet music, records, tapes and CDs; the right to perform your song for an audience; the right to display your written song in public; the right to lease your song; the right to will your song to your heirs; and the right to decide who will record your song first. As the songwriter, you are the only person entitled to these rights, unless you wrote your song for hire or in collaboration with someone else. You alone can provide others with permission to use your song.

Q: Are you entitled to these same protections if your song was written for hire?
A: No. If you were hired to write a song (a jingle for a product or business, for example), the person or business that hired you controls the copyright. If you have any questions about your rights to the song, you should check your contract with the company that hired you.

Q: Is it true that you do not have to register your song to receive protection under the copyright law?
A: Technically, it is true that registration is not necessary. The law states that as soon as the song is finished (that is, as soon as it is either written down or recorded), it is automatically protected.

Q: Why should you register your song, then?
A: Although copyright registration does not actually provide additional protection for a song, the fact that you created an original song on a certain date becomes a matter of public record as soon as the song is registered with the Library of Congress. This makes it easier to sue if someone uses your song without permission because there will be no question about the date you created the song. In addition, if your song is registered, you will be able to sue for statutory damages—set penalties established by law—rather than just suing for the amount of money you lost due to the other person's unauthorized use of your song. (It is harder to prove that you have lost money than it is to prove that someone has violated the copyright law.) Also, if your song is registered, you are more likely to be reimbursed for your lawyer's fees as part of a lawsuit settlement.

Q: What if you have a song that you finished years ago, but never registered? Is it too late?
A: No, you can register a song at anytime. The registration date, however, will reflect the date you filled out the form, not the date you completed the song.

Q: Do you have to wait until your song has been published or released to register it?
A: No. You can register your song as soon as it is written down or recorded.

Q: What is the first thing you need to do to register?
A: You must fill out an application form, which can be obtained from the Copyright Office of the Library of Congress. Usually, to register an original song, you will need Form PA (see sample, pages 23-24). This form is for the registration of published or unpublished works of the performing arts. You can register both your music and your lyrics through this form by following the detailed instructions that come with the form.

Q: How can you get a form?
A: You can get a form by calling the twenty-four-hour Copyright Office Hotline at (202) 707-9100 and leaving a message on the recorder. Once you have received a form, you are permitted to photocopy it if you want to register more than one song. The photocopy must be on good grade white 8½″ × 11″ paper that can be fed automatically through a photocopier.

Q: How long will it take the copyright office to mail you your form?
A: It usually takes two to three weeks.

Q: How much does it cost to register your song?
A: As of January 3, 1991, the registration fee is $20. You must mail a check or money order, payable to Register of Copyrights, covering this fee. The $10 fee was raised to $20 when the copyright act was amended in 1990. The fees are due for another adjustment in January 1995.

Q: What should you send with the form and the check or money order?
A: If your work has not yet been published, you must send one complete copy or phonorecord (record, tape or CD) of your work. If the work has been published, you must send two complete copies or one phonorecord of the best edition. If your work was first published outside the United States, you must send one complete copy or phonorecord of the first foreign edition. If you have contributed to a collective work (i.e., a musical, etc.), you must send one complete copy or phonorecord of the best edition of the collective work. These are called deposits.

Q: Where should you send the form?
A: The form should be sent to the following address: Register of Copyrights, Copyright Office, Library of Congress, Washington DC 20559.

Q: How do you register a song written in collaboration with someone else? What about the songs used in a musical for which someone else wrote the libretto?
A: There is space on Form PA to list all the collaborators. When a collaborated work is copyrighted, the copyright is owned by all the collaborators.

Q: Where can you get more information about registering your song?
A: You can call the Copyright Office's Public Information Office at (202) 707-3000. Recorded information is available twenty-four hours a day, seven days a week, but if you want to talk to someone, you must call between 8:30 A.M. and 5:00 P.M. Eastern Time, Monday-Friday.

Q: What if you don't want to pay $20 for every song you write? Is there any way around this?
A: You can register a group of songs under one copyright by placing them together in a packet and naming the collection (for example, Joe Smoe's Songs, 1993). This title alone will appear on the official registration papers. (Names of individual songs will not.) To register a compilation of songs, you must have written all of them by yourself. While the Copyright Office will keep every song in your compilation on file, this method of registration is slightly more risky than registering each individual song, because authorship is more difficult to prove this way.

Q: What if you change your song after it has been registered?
A: You can re-register the song by filling out Form PA again and specifying on line six that you are registering a derivative work.

Q: How long does the registration stay on file? Will you need to renew it?
A: That depends on when you wrote your song. In a nutshell, here are the general laws pertaining to length of copyright protection:

For songs written after January 1, 1978—If you wrote your song after January 1, 1978 (when amendments to the 1909 copyright law went into effect), you do not need to renew your registration. Your song is protected until fifty years after you have died; then, it goes into the public domain.

For songs written between January 1, 1964, and December 31, 1977—A 1992 law makes renewal optional for songs copyrighted between January 1, 1964, and December 31, 1977. The copyrights on these songs will be automatically renewed, and the copyright will last until fifty years after your death. However, even though the copyright automatically renews itself, if you do not file to renew your registration, you forfeit any statutory damages and attorney fees if you win a copyright infringement suit.

For songs written before January 1, 1964—If your song was written before January 1, 1964, your copyright is effective for twenty-eight years after the date of registration, at which time the copyright must be renewed. The renewal lasts for an additional forty-seven years, so if you renew your copyright, it is good for a total of seventy-five years.

Q: How long does the registration process take?
A: Although the registration date will reflect the date you filled out the form, and not the date your form was processed, you should hear from the copyright office within sixteen weeks. You will either receive a certificate of registration, a letter stating that your request for registration has been denied, or a phone call or letter asking you to clarify some information. Because of the volume of mail the copyright office receives each day, the office cannot answer questions about the status of your application over the phone before sixteen weeks have passed. If you want to make sure that the office receives your form, send it registered or certified mail, and request a receipt. Even if you do this, however, you should wait at least three weeks to receive the receipt.

Q: What if you need proof of registration before the form has been processed?
A: You have to pay a fee if you need information about your application for registration before sixteen weeks have passed. Call the Copyright Office at (202) 707-3000 for more information.

Q: When your song is published, what happens to the copyright? Is it still solely yours?
A: That depends on your contract with the publisher, so read it carefully before signing. The standard procedure is that when your song is published,

you agree to share the copyright with the publisher. If your contract follows this procedure, you can request to have the full copyright returned to you thirty-five years after the song is published. Any royalties your song earns thirty-five or more years after it is published will revert to you. Be wary of contracts where the publisher receives sole control of the copyright at the time of publication; if you sign a contract like this, you are actually giving away your song or selling it outright.

Q: Can you sue a person for infringement of copyright and receive compensation even if the person has not made any money by using your song?
A: Yes. You can sue the person for statutory damages—damages that are set by law for breaking the copyright laws—as long as your song is registered. If your song has not been registered, you cannot be compensated for statutory damages and can sue only for the money the individual has made from the sale or performance of your song. Check with your lawyer for more technical information regarding a lawsuit.

Q: What can you do if someone steals the title of your song?
A: The copyright laws do not protect titles.

Q: What can you do if you think someone has stolen the theme or idea of your song?
A: The copyright laws do not protect ideas.

Q: What if only a small part of a song's melody sounds similar, or a few lines of your lyrics are used in a song that otherwise does not resemble your song at all? Can you still sue?
A: You must be able to prove that the song has "substantial similarity" to the song you wrote. The two tests that a court uses to prove this are (1) expert witnesses must testify that the melodic construction and the general idea is the same and (2) after listening to both songs, a jury must decide whether they sound alike or close enough that one could be mistaken for another. There is no particular number of bars, words or notes that can be legally copied, so each case is unique.

Q: Do you give up any rights to your song when you give someone permission to use it?
A: No. Granting permission to use your work does not affect your rights to a song. As long as you own the copyright, you retain all rights to the song. When you give someone permission to use the song, you are still entitled to the writer's share of any revenue the song makes.

SAMPLE COPYRIGHT FORM PA

FORM PA
For a Work of the Performing Arts
UNITED STATES COPYRIGHT OFFICE

REGISTRATION NUMBER

PA   PAU

EFFECTIVE DATE OF REGISTRATION

Month   Day   Year

DO NOT WRITE ABOVE THIS LINE. IF YOU NEED MORE SPACE, USE A SEPARATE CONTINUATION SHEET.

1

TITLE OF THIS WORK ▼

PREVIOUS OR ALTERNATIVE TITLES ▼

NATURE OF THIS WORK ▼ See instructions

2 a

NAME OF AUTHOR ▼

DATES OF BIRTH AND DEATH
Year Born ▼   Year Died ▼

Was this contribution to the work a "work made for hire"?
☐ Yes
☐ No

AUTHOR'S NATIONALITY OR DOMICILE
Name of Country
OR { Citizen of ▶
Domiciled in▶

WAS THIS AUTHOR'S CONTRIBUTION TO THE WORK
Anonymous? ☐ Yes ☐ No
Pseudonymous? ☐ Yes ☐ No

If the answer to either of these questions is "Yes," see detailed instructions.

NATURE OF AUTHORSHIP   Briefly describe nature of material created by this author in which copyright is claimed. ▼

NOTE

Under the law, the "author" of a "work made for hire" is generally the employer, not the employee (see instructions). For any part of this work that was "made for hire" check "Yes" in the space provided, give the employer (or other person for whom the work was prepared) as "Author" of that part, and leave the space for dates of birth and death blank.

b

NAME OF AUTHOR ▼

DATES OF BIRTH AND DEATH
Year Born ▼   Year Died ▼

Was this contribution to the work a "work made for hire"?
☐ Yes
☐ No

AUTHOR'S NATIONALITY OR DOMICILE
Name of Country
OR { Citizen of ▶
Domiciled in▶

WAS THIS AUTHOR'S CONTRIBUTION TO THE WORK
Anonymous? ☐ Yes ☐ No
Pseudonymous? ☐ Yes ☐ No

If the answer to either of these questions is "Yes," see detailed instructions.

NATURE OF AUTHORSHIP   Briefly describe nature of material created by this author in which copyright is claimed. ▼

c

NAME OF AUTHOR ▼

DATES OF BIRTH AND DEATH
Year Born ▼   Year Died ▼

Was this contribution to the work a "work made for hire"?
☐ Yes
☐ No

AUTHOR'S NATIONALITY OR DOMICILE
Name of Country
OR { Citizen of ▶
Domiciled in▶

WAS THIS AUTHOR'S CONTRIBUTION TO THE WORK
Anonymous? ☐ Yes ☐ No
Pseudonymous? ☐ Yes ☐ No

If the answer to either of these questions is "Yes," see detailed instructions.

NATURE OF AUTHORSHIP   Briefly describe nature of material created by this author in which copyright is claimed. ▼

3 a

YEAR IN WHICH CREATION OF THIS WORK WAS COMPLETED   This information must be given ◀Year in all cases.

b DATE AND NATION OF FIRST PUBLICATION OF THIS PARTICULAR WORK
Complete this information ONLY if this work has been published.
Month▶   Day▶   Year▶   ◀ Nation

4

See instructions before completing this space.

COPYRIGHT CLAIMANT(S) Name and address must be given even if the claimant is the same as the author given in space 2. ▼

TRANSFER If the claimant(s) named here in space 4 is (are) different from the author(s) named in space 2, give a brief statement of how the claimant(s) obtained ownership of the copyright. ▼

DO NOT WRITE HERE OFFICE USE ONLY

APPLICATION RECEIVED

ONE DEPOSIT RECEIVED

TWO DEPOSITS RECEIVED

FUNDS RECEIVED

MORE ON BACK ▶   • Complete all applicable spaces (numbers 5-9) on the reverse side of this page.
   • See detailed instructions.   • Sign the form at line 8.

DO NOT WRITE HERE
Page 1 of _____ pages

Be sure to use the most recent form. Instructions for completing the form will accompany it

EXAMINED BY	FORM PA
CHECKED BY	
☐ CORRESPONDENCE Yes	FOR COPYRIGHT OFFICE USE ONLY

DO NOT WRITE ABOVE THIS LINE. IF YOU NEED MORE SPACE, USE A SEPARATE CONTINUATION SHEET.

PREVIOUS REGISTRATION Has registration for this work, or for an earlier version of this work, already been made in the Copyright Office?
☐ Yes ☐ No If your answer is "Yes," why is another registration being sought? (Check appropriate box) ▼
a. ☐ This is the first published edition of a work previously registered in unpublished form.
b. ☐ This is the first application submitted by this author as copyright claimant.
c. ☐ This is a changed version of the work, as shown by space 6 on this application.
If your answer is "Yes," give: **Previous Registration Number ▼**   **Year of Registration ▼**

5

DERIVATIVE WORK OR COMPILATION Complete both space 6a and 6b for a derivative work; complete only 6b for a compilation.
a. Preexisting Material Identify any preexisting work or works that this work is based on or incorporates. ▼

b. Material Added to This Work Give a brief, general statement of the material that has been added to this work and in which copyright is claimed. ▼

6

See instructions before completing this space.

DEPOSIT ACCOUNT If the registration fee is to be charged to a Deposit Account established in the Copyright Office, give name and number of Account.
Name ▼   **Account Number ▼**

CORRESPONDENCE Give name and address to which correspondence about this application should be sent.   Name/Address/Apt/City/State/ZIP ▼

Area Code and Telephone Number ▶

7

Be sure to give your daytime phone number ◀

CERTIFICATION* I, the undersigned, hereby certify that I am the
Check only one ▼
☐ author
☐ other copyright claimant
☐ owner of exclusive right(s)
☐ authorized agent of _____
                Name of author or other copyright claimant, or owner of exclusive right(s) ▲

of the work identified in this application and that the statements made
by me in this application are correct to the best of my knowledge.

Typed or printed name and date ▼ If this application gives a date of publication in space 3, do not sign and submit it before that date.
                                                                    date ▶ _____

☞   Handwritten signature (X) ▼

8

MAIL CERTIFICATE TO

Name ▼

Number/Street/Apartment Number ▼

Certificate will be mailed in window envelope

City/State/ZIP ▼

YOU MUST
• Complete all necessary spaces
• Sign your application in space 8
SEND ALL 3 ELEMENTS IN THE SAME PACKAGE
1. Application form
2. Nonrefundable $20 filing fee in check or money order payable to *Register of Copyrights*
3. Deposit material
MAIL TO
Register of Copyrights
Library of Congress
Washington, D.C. 20559-6000

The Copyright Office has the authority to adjust fees at 5-year intervals, based on changes in the Consumer Price Index. The next adjustment is due in 1996. Please contact the Copyright Office after July 1995 to determine the actual fee schedule.

9

*17 U.S.C. § 506(e): Any person who knowingly makes a false representation of a material fact in the application for copyright registration provided for by section 409, or in any written statement filed in connection with the application, shall be fined not more than $2,500.

July 1993—400,000   ♻ PRINTED ON RECYCLED PAPER   ☆U.S. GOVERNMENT PRINTING OFFICE: 1993-342-582/80,018

Don't forget to reread these important steps

CHAPTER 4

MANAGERS AND BOOKING AGENTS

Nothing begets success like success. If your act is performing locally, garnering some decent press, expanding your following, and generally making a little noise, odds are that you'll be met by a variety of people who wish to attach themselves to your gravy train. But be careful. Your manager and your agent will play key roles in your success as a musician. If you want to be successful, you must be well informed in order to choose a manager and an agent who are right for you.

THE MANAGER'S JOB

Managers are probably one of the most important, yet least understood functionaries in the music business. Technically, a manager is employed by an artist to act on his or her behalf. The manager also heads up the support team, which includes the lawyer, agent and business manager, and is responsible for the coalition of all elements of his client's career. The manager is also responsible for long-term career plans and aspects of financial planning, along with the business manager.

In addition to business functions, a manager acts as a buffer between the artist and the cold realities of the real world. The manager fields requests for time and money and acts as a confidant, partner, psychologist and cheerleader. Since management is very much a personal business, involvement in the artist's life is an important factor. For many beginning performers, the function of manager is often assumed by a friend who has some concept of business, publicity, marketing and, hopefully, music. Beginning bands or artists can be aided by having someone else take care of their business (or at least appear to) since it increases their credibility. Because your manager represents you in all dealings, always be sure to discuss every business move, decision and venture completely, and never assume that your manager knows more than you do. Educating yourself about the music business is crucial. There is a language and a code to be learned. A good manager can work with you to learn the ropes.

There are legal limits to how much responsibility a manager can take on. In California, managers are prohibited by law from actually obtaining work for clients. They may function strictly in an advisory position, though they are permitted to negotiate recording contracts on their client's behalf. This statute is meant to differentiate the role of the manager from that of the agent, who books entertainers into venues for performances. It is not possible, therefore, for someone to be both a manager and an agent. However, some managers still get work for their clients, although they are prohibited by law from doing so. Beginning performers often spend more money than is coming in, creating negative cash flow. At this point, managers can invest in their act, usually for a share of the profits if the act is signed to a record deal. This is not mandatory in a managerial relationship, but it does occur.

THE MANAGER'S CONTRACT

Successful managers are rewarded handsomely for their time, expertise and efforts. Payment comes from gross receipts of records, tours, merchandising, publishing and ancillary income. Fifteen to twenty percent of gross income is considered a standard fee, though no rules apply. Many managers actually reduce their percentage the higher their client's income. However, Elvis Presley's long-time manager, Colonel Tom Parker, helped himself to 50 percent of the king's assets for many years.

The term length for a personal manager can be from three to five years, but artists often prefer a shorter term in case the relationship doesn't work to the artist's satisfaction. There should be minimum performance standards to warrant renewing a contract with a manager: Either certain goals must be achieved or a minimum earning standard. It is generally the artist's decision to renew with his management company, and contracts don't renew automatically. Surprisingly, many managers, even superstar ones, prefer to work without a contract. Kenny Rogers' manager, Ken Kragen, has had a handshake deal with Rogers for twenty odd years. He feels that if the only bond between a manager and an artist is on paper, then the relationship is not a fruitful nor trusting one and should be reevaluated. Usually, as long as the manager properly represents his client's interests, all is harmonious.

HOW TO CHOOSE A MANAGER

Since the first person a potential record company, booking agent, music periodical, publishing company, etc., sees is your manager, make sure that he or she is the correct person to properly advance your musical vision. Expertise in other businesses does not necessarily translate to success in the music business. If someone presents themselves to you as a potential manager, don't be hypnotized by symbols of wealth or promises of fame; take your time in making this vital decision.

Since proper career moves are particularly crucial for the beginning artist, make sure that your manager shares your artistic vision. If you're a hard-core rap group, for instance, you obviously wouldn't choose a manager whose expertise lies in working with lounge acts from your local Holiday Inn.

For an example of what can happen, take this brilliant singer/songwriter that lived in New York City. He had a rough-hewn charm and a literary bent that showed through his music, lyrics and presentation. Under the misguided direction of his manager (the first one he'd ever worked with), he was soon adorned in a tuxedo, singing cabaret songs in front of a bored band for patrons of upper east side dining establishments—an audience that his manager most identified with. This unlikely duo eventually went their separate ways, but the singer had tarnished his reputation and lost valuable time. He never regained his footing or his original inspiration. Don't let this happen to you.

THE AGENT'S JOB

Agents in the music business are involved in touring and performing, but don't participate in the fields of songwriting or recording. If you're a successful recording act, your agent will work with your personal manager and concert promoters to set up lucrative tours in different national and international markets. Agents' terms for this type of arrangement are generally one year, and they take a standard 10 percent of the gross income for efforts related to live performances. For the local or regional band, agents generally book parties, clubs and concerts. Successful agents working on this level may have acts of different types. They may also book a specific club or chain of clubs on a regular or exclusive basis, or they may have a handle on the lucrative corporate or casual scene. In the case of all agents at all levels though, keep one thought firmly in mind: *The agent's primary loyalty is to his buyer, not to the talent.* Talent changes, but buyers remain consistent for longer periods of time, and it's the buyer who pays the agent, though indirectly.

In California, as mentioned previously, managers are prohibited by law from finding work for their clients, so an agent fulfills this function. To be an agent in California, the applicant must post a $10,000 bond and be recognized by the state: a practice that separates the fly-by-nighters from the big boys quite handily. An agent, as a middleman, will be most interested in what slots he can fit you into to accrue instant or immediate income for himself.

Do all of your research before contacting an agent. Find out what he books, who he handles, what types of acts he specializes in and if he will listen to your work. Some agents don't represent clients on an exclusive basis, and it is possible to be signed to more than one agent, particularly on the local or regional level. If an agent will only work with you on an exclusive basis, however, make sure that he's indeed the correct agent for you and can keep you working continually. Keep the contract as short as possible, preferably one year or less, with an option for renewal pursuant to your evaluation of his success in booking you.

When choosing an agent, use the same considerations you used when choosing a manager. If you're an industrial trash/funk band, don't go with an agent who books heart-shaped bathtub resorts for honeymooners in the Poconos. Be selective. You can be sure that the successful agent will be.

THE SUBMISSION PACKAGE OR PRESS KIT

The most advantageous time to look for management is when your career has gained some momentum. Below is a list of questions to ask yourself before submitting:

1. Have I taken my career as far as I can on my own?
2. Am I generating income that would make me attractive to an agent or a manager?
3. Can I explain who my target audience is?
4. What empirical information can I provide to support my marketability to this audience?
5. Can I describe my act in five words or less?
6. Is my audiotape radio ready?
7. Is my videotape 100 percent representative of my show? (If you have to apologize for anything you're presenting, don't present it; redo it instead).
8. Are my pictures current?
9. Are all materials legible, neat and professional?
10. Am I confident that I can sell myself effectively?
11. Can I deliver the goods once I've opened the door?

When you are sure you are ready to present yourself, you must compile a submission package, often called a press kit by managers, which includes a letter, a black-and-white photo, a bio, your name and logo, a demo tape and, sometimes, a videotape. Business cards and personalized stationery can also be included. The press kit is the first piece of information a prospective manager or agent will receive about you, so it must look professional.

The Letter
The first element, of course, is your letter. See chapters five through ten for tips on writing the letter and see the samples on pages 38-40 of this chapter.

Remember these simple guidelines:

1. Keep it short!
2. Don't use superlatives ("The greatest, the best")
3. Follow up within a week after sending. If your contact has received it but hasn't reviewed it, your calls can be a gentle reminder to do so.
4. Persistence is good; abrasion is not.
5. Don't be oversolicitous in correspondence.
6. Don't be too casual—when in doubt, generally the more conservative approach to letter writing is preferred.
7. Agents are buyers and sellers; keep to commerce, not art.
8. Let the music sell itself.

The Photograph

You'll need a professional black-and-white picture. Good photographers don't come cheap. Three hundred fifty dollars is standard in Los Angeles for a couple of rolls of black and white, a contact sheet and maybe one or two 8×10s. Your selection should include both studio and action shots. It is vital that the photographer understands the type of music that you're creating and has heard it so the picture will best represent what you do. Keep in mind that a potential buyer of talent or prospective audience member who doesn't know anything about a band or a singer should have some idea about what the act does from only seeing it represented in a black-and-white photo. Be sure to select at least one print that will look good in a newspaper or newsprint format also; since thousands of readers see these mediums of print, make your efforts count. Use common sense and plan your shot, with different outfits, props and locations. Wear clothing that compliments and represents what you do, and consult friends whose opinions you trust. Don't include anything that would make a potential manager question your taste or your sanity. Bare mid-riffs and glistening pecs are great if the singer spends long hours in the gym, and if the music is equally muscular, but use some restraint (not to be confused with conservatism) and a modicum of taste.

Bios

"Bio" is short for biography and is a short sketch of your recent past, your current accomplishments and your future. Never include a bio of over two pages, since it won't get read. Less is more, so keep it concise and to the point. Make sure that your bio is directly related to information concerning your music, since the reader won't care about much else. Above all:

1. Make the truth sound as good as possible.
2. Keep your reader well entertained.

The more the reader is entertained, the better the chance that he'll actually read your bio and come away with a positive impression of what he is about to hear.

Superlatives have a place, but not in your bio or your press materials. Describing your band as "the best" or "the greatest" is a real turn-off and probably not true. Just as you do when writing a song or a poem: Make every word count.

Typewritten and offset copies of your bio materials are acceptable, but access to a computer and a laser printer can really make your written words shine. Never hand print a bio. Always make sure there are no misspellings and that punctuation, grammar and syntax are correct. Don't change subjects or possessives halfway through the page. Have a knowledgeable person proofread all of your materials, or if using a computer word processing program, call up your trusty spell-checker. Sloppy cross-outs, misspelled words, cheap copies, smeared printing and bad quality paper represent the misguided efforts of amateurs. Since the person receiving your press kit begins making judgments about your act immediately, make the press kit count.

Either as a part of your bio, or as another separate piece, list recent performances of your act. Reviews of your shows, newspaper and magazine articles are a real plus, but make sure that they're duplicated legibly and professionally. If you have a number of reviews or articles, you may want to duplicate only a few in complete form and pull quotes from the others to print on a single page. This is also a handy way to keep the good and chop out the bad. And since a press kit is not a legal document, it lends itself to creativity. See also sample bios on pages 49-51.

Business Cards

A business card (see sample, page 37) is a convenient way to keep your contact information always on hand for potential managers or agents. Keep them tasteful and simple. Don't use needlessly distracting graphics or ugly type styles. Avoid using the hideous "Olde English" font (unless maybe you represent heavy metal bands), nor any other font that makes the reader wonder if he should have his eyes checked. The card stock doesn't have to be fancy. Glossy is nice if it's within your budget, but don't use the holographic, ribbed, rainbow or affected look. A well-designed logo can add to a card, but avoid the tacky standard "clip art," such as music note designs, that your printer probably has in a book he hasn't changed since 1956.

Computers and laser printers can be an asset if you're designing your own card; you can set the type, then take the camera-ready card to your duplicating facility. This will allow you to experiment with your creation before you commit it to boxes of product.

Finally, never cross out a telephone number. If you're going to be moving often, get cards without phone numbers and then write the numbers in as needed. Cross-outs are easily read signposts of amateurs.

Logos. Most big-time acts have a logo, or specially designed written representations of their names. A logo can be used on stationery, posters, flyers, pictures, stage backdrops and T-shirts. Although logo designers are well-paid specialists, the revolution of computer art and graphics have put logo design in the hands of the computer user. Maybe a friend or acquaintance who attends a design school and actually knows your music could design a better logo for you than someone with more experience who doesn't. A logo is useless unless it can be read by the naked eye, preferably from a distance for onstage use. All elements of your press kit should bear your logo. Copies should be made for every conceivable use and, if you're using computers, have a copy of your logo scanned for use on computer-generated materials. Have veloxes made also: These are high-quality prints on shiny sturdy paper, which you can then paste on your materials when you have them copied.

Band and Artist Names. Of course, on the business card, you'll have the name of your group. Naming your act is directly related to your future success. It must reflect your music. Think of it as a brand name, one that would interest and attract the buyer at first glance. Product names, such as Roach Motel, Tide, Pledge, etc., deliver a specific set of responses from a supermarket shelf, billboard or television set. Likewise, U2, Metallica and Guns 'n' Roses deliver a concise picture of the music that these acts create. For the solo act, sincerely devote some time to the decision of keeping or changing your family name. Robert Zimmerman (Bob Dylan) and David Jones (David Bowie) changed their names to make themselves more marketable. On the other hand, Bruce Springsteen, Bruce Hornsby and John Cougar Mellencamp (who incorporated the moniker that an early manager gave him) all kept their family names. Single name acts like Hammer, Madonna and Prince have the advantage of being most easily remembered.

Cassette Tapes

For music acts, a cassette tape is crucial to your press kit. In chapter one you read a detailed account of putting together the best possible demo tape, so I won't duplicate that information, but your labeling of the tape, your tape box, your J-card and, of course, the music is your bottom line. You will definitely be prejudged on your music if:

1. You use a ninety-minute tape for three songs.
2. Your label is sloppy, badly printed or some ghastly color (unless this is a part of your marketing scheme).
3. Your tape box is scratched, cracked or fingerprinted.

The same rules apply to your videotape if you present one. Make sure to have custom labels printed for both audio- and videotape; have your phone number and, if possible, a logo on absolutely everything.

Lyric sheets are not essential in press kits; however, if the lyrics to an act's songs are vital to the image or marketing strategy, they can be included. Consider reducing them to fit on one page if they can still be read at that size. Never include lead sheets or chord sheets (see sample sheets in chapter two, pages 13-17).

"Video Killed the Radio Star"

In 1981, a whole new era in rock and roll began with the formation of MTV, Music Television. Originally presenting only videos, the network has since widened its format, but the primary focus remains video presentations of songs, twenty-four hours a day. Video can be a boon to the act looking for representation from either a manager or an agent. In the case of an agency that books clubs or casuals, the agent may want to use a video when presenting an act to potential buyers. Since video is so accessible to amateurs, there is a tendency to overvideo, particularly live performance. Although it is much easier for an agent or manager to review potential signings in the privacy of his office, he certainly won't want to sit through a taped hour-and-a-half set. Keep your presentation concise; one or two songs should do it.

Live performance videos can be very strong, but not for all styles or acts. Some acts are better heard than seen—in that case, the use of a video can be downright damaging. Musicians are not necessarily actors. If you don't have the visual appeal, don't be forced into an uncomfortable situation; find another way to let your music speak.

Soundwise, video doesn't have the capabilities of flexible multitrack recording, unless an act has a mobile recording truck present (a very expensive proposition). Certain types of music lose their impact on the small screen—especially rock and roll, so keep the images interesting, using different angles, and if possible, more than one camera. If you opt for the MTV impressionistic form, avoid these clichés: dry ice, smoke machines and women in cages. Make sure that your music and images are in sync with the soundtrack also. Higher ticket videos are usually shot on 16mm film, edited in this format, and then transferred to video. Shooting directly to video can establish a certain immediacy, especially if using ¾" industrial tape.

Although big-budget videos typically run in the $100,000-and-up bracket, a band with a little ingenuity can produce a watchable video for around $1,000. Schools, colleges and recording schools usually have film and television production classes. Try becoming someone's pet project and work with them to produce a visual representation of your music. An inspired friend with video equipment can be a strong ally in the production of your visual image.

The same care must be shown in packaging videotape as in audio; make sure your box, label and sticker are top of the line. Always put your phone number on everything!

Binders

The most common binders for press kits are 8½″×11″ folders with inside pockets. They can be different colors or adorned and printed with your act's name. An example of an effective and striking press kit might use a white glossy folder with a color photocopy of the act's name attached via a permanent spray or fixative to the front of the folders. Folders retail for about $1.00 each, but they are a little cheaper if bought in bulk from a stationery supply store.

Sliding a cassette tape or a videotape into a folder can be a little awkward. Another alternative is Pitch-A-Pak—presentation folders specifically designed to hold cassettes and videos. The product is available from sheet music stores, or directly from the company. You can write them for information. Send an SASE to Pitch-A-Pak, P.O. Box 566, Reseda, CA 91337, or call (818) 772-6941.

When sending press kits by mail, always use bubble envelopes to protect your materials. These cost about $1.29 or so, but are lightweight and keep the corners of your folders and tapes from tearing through the envelope. Always use typewritten stickers, preferably with your logo, and make sure that you know the correct name, title and spelling of the person you're writing. If you've put together a professional, striking visual package for your act, the chance that your package will be looked at and ultimately listened to is very high.

Stationery

Any music-related business needs stationery with the company name or logo, telephone number, address and FAX number, if applicable. Again, the object is to unify every element of your presentation, so go for the better bond stationery. Avoid trendy colors and make sure that your typewriter or printer is adaptable to the type of paper you're using. White, off-white, wheat and oyster grey stationery give a professional and easily readable impression. Your company name/logo can be at the top of the page, the right corner or the bottom, whichever position works best with the art. Matching envelopes are a nice touch, preferably embossed with your company name.

A laser printer can be used to design your own stationery. You can then take the master to a printer to have it reproduced. Whether you purchase the stationery or design it yourself, remember that readability is the most important consideration.

LIVE SHOWCASES

A performance specifically geared to presenting an act to potential buyers is commonly referred to as a showcase. An agent, especially, will usually want to see you perform live to determine your adaptability and performance skills and see how well you fit his particular set of needs.

Although live showcases can be presented in a club, often they are more like miniconcerts. The main objective is to make your act look and sound as good as possible, and the more control you can exert over these factors in presenting your show, the better the result. If you have access to the rental of a small theater in your area, this can be a good alternative to the smoke-filled environment of a club. You can also bring in your own sound and hopefully use the lights of the theater to coordinate a professionally staged visual show. In the case of a controlled venue showcase performance, invite your buyers and enough fans and friends so that the room doesn't feel empty. Try to overcome the artificiality of the situation and be natural. Yelling "howya doin' Toledo" to ten people won't work.

If you do present your act in a club and invite the individuals you want to impress, make sure that the sound and lights are exactly what you want; insist on a sound and technical check. In Los Angeles, pay to play is the rule. A promoter books three or four bands per night and sells them advance tickets, which they in turn must sell or give away (at $10 or so a pop) to their friends, family and fans. Since each band pays approximately $800 to $1,000 (times three or four bands), the promoter usually does all right. Add to this the cost of paying the sound and light man and, sometimes, for rental of the dressing rooms, and you have some idea of the economics involved.

Rather than condemn this practice (which many bands do), it's important to find alternatives. Since so many bands follow the same routes, there is little press appeal in doing the same old thing. Outdoor festivals, street fairs and other cultural and community events have the advantage of higher visibility. You'll be playing for larger and more diverse audiences than the friends you can cajole to come down and see your act at a high-priced club. Benefit performances are also a great way for agents and managers to see your act. Capitalizing your press on top of an event's can give you credibility and exposure that you'd never obtain in years of performing at clubs.

This is all about show biz; every element of your live performance must be coordinated in order to look professional. Live performance is a great way to sell your act—but don't follow other's well-worn paths. Your creativity and your originality are the keys to your future. Let it come from the heart.

SUBMITTING MATERIALS TO MANAGERS FOR A SPECIFIC ARTIST

Getting your songs in front of recording artists can be difficult. Many artists and major record companies no longer accept unsolicited materials. The reason for this is simple: Record companies were sued so often that is was easier to remove this potential form of aggravation from their business. It is possible, however, to use a management office to submit materials if the writer follows the guidelines for submissions, knows his song is perfect and presents himself professionally.

Timing is important. It is essential to know when the artist is recording, when they are in preproduction for the album and when they will be reviewing material. Typically, artists begin working on albums at least a year before they see the light of release. The artist looks for material at least a month before the recording process begins.

You will need to track this information through music trade magazines, such as *Billboard*, or by calling the management office. Be sure that the artist records outside material and that you have a song that is consistent with the new album project, not a clone of a song on the last album.

Keep in mind that many artists don't make the final decisions on what they record. The artists and repertoire (A&R) department of their record label, and especially their producer, make the ultimate decision.

On page 38, there is a sample letter to a management company for the purpose of submitting a song for an artist. Always address such a letter directly to the manager. Again, as with any submission, make sure your phone number, name and address are prominent on the package. If the Mahalos like the song and intend to record it, the publishing information may be crucial to making the deal if the band requires the writer to assign a percentage of the publishing revenues to them.

In the rock and roll arena, most bands write their own material. This is not always so much an artistic decision as an economic one; the band will make considerably more money from songs on which they control the copyrights. However, one superstar British artist writes very few of his best-known hits, but his name appears on songs as a co-writer. This is a continuation of the 1950s way of doing business: A songwriter, in order to ensure that his song would be recorded, would allow the recording artist to be listed as a co-writer, thus giving up 50 percent of his income. This practice is no longer common and should not be condoned.

TELEPHONE TOOLS

Blindly calling or submitting to agents or managers is a waste of time, postage and money spent on the phone bill. If you have done your homework, established yourself, built up your credibility in your local market and have a plan, then it may be time to contact agents or managers. First, contact the manager or agent's office to inquire into their submission policies for new acts. Many times you'll be given the standard answer "we're not accepting new clients at this moment." Think of this response as the moment when the fun begins, because now it's up to you to say the right thing to open the door back up.

Speaking with a manager or agent's secretary may be the most important conversation you'll ever have, because it's up to them (the gatekeepers, as they're called) to decide whether or not you'll ever speak with their bosses. Always treat them with as much respect as you'd give their employers. Learn their names and the best times to contact them and be respectful of their time on the phone. If you keep getting the response "we're not accepting material at this time," ask if you can submit directly to them. Odds are that if your presentation is on the money they'll be glad to submit it on your behalf to their superiors—it could make them look good, too. When submitting materials, make sure you've done your homework: You should know who is with the company, who reviews materials (gather this information in your original phone call) and how to pronounce the names. This may seem obvious, but a letter or package sent "To whom it may concern" will certainly wind up in the circular file of any reputable company.

To attract the interest of agents and managers, presell your name and establish yourself in their minds before you submit to them. Make them the target of your mailings (see sample letters, pages 39-40); send them brief notes inviting them to your local shows. They may actually attend (prepare yourself for that possibility by giving an RSVP number for your guest list), but even if they don't, they'll see your name. Send periodic press releases and performance reviews also.

FOLLOWING UP ON SUBMISSIONS

One of the hardest parts of the submissions process is following up on submission packages. To track your submissions, use a large calendar to mark all correspondence, dates of follow-up calls and dates when to make the calls. Within one week after sending out a tape/video or press kit, make your initial follow-up call. Ostensibly, this call is simply to find out if the materials were received; however, the real purpose is to cement your name in the recipient's mind and to remind them to look at/watch/listen to your package. The call is also to show them that you mean business.

A word about music industry communication habits: Since the music business is often viewed as a hard-bitten world (and for damn good reason), there is no need to adopt a pushy or obnoxious persona. Indeed, good manners, a personable phone voice, a sense of timing (always ask or determine whether the person to whom you're speaking is pressured for time; if so, ask if you can call them at a better time) are valuable. Maintain a sense of humor on the phone. Put a mirror near your phone and monitor your facial expressions during your phone calls. A smile can actually be heard over the phone, so make yourself smile, and often. If you have trouble reaching someone at the management office or agency, try calling in the early evening hours after the secretaries have left; you may be surprised who answers the phone.

CONCLUSION

No one is going to appear out of the woodwork to make you a star. You cannot be magically transported from playing air guitar in front of the mirror in your bedroom to the vat super-trooper lit stage of Madison Square Garden. There is only one person who must provide the initiative, musical talent, vision, money, creativity and motivation to make your career happen, and that person is you.

In show business, particularly the music business, rules are made to be broken, and there is no single agenda that must be adhered to. Indeed, chutzpah and innovation are key concepts. Good luck in submitting, and don't give up!

SAMPLE BUSINESS CARD

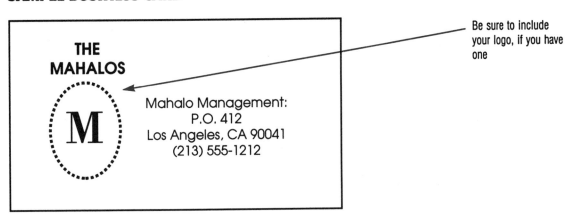

Be sure to include your logo, if you have one

SAMPLE SUBMISSION LETTER TO A MANAGEMENT COMPANY

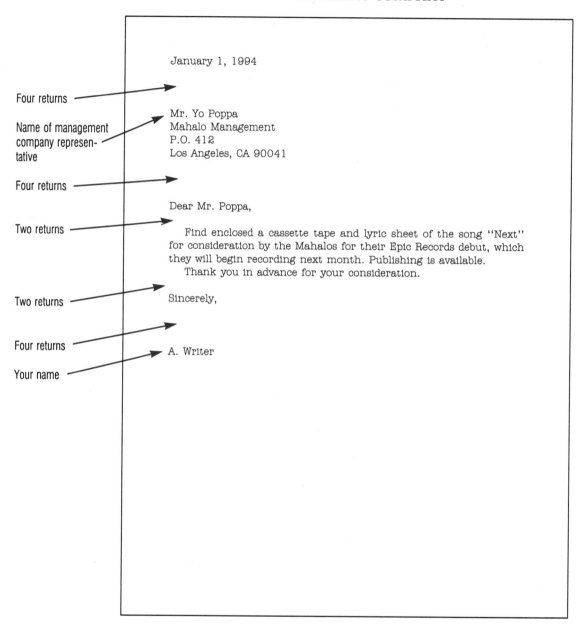

January 1, 1994

Four returns ⟶

Name of management
company represen-
tative ⟶

Mr. Yo Poppa
Mahalo Management
P.O. 412
Los Angeles, CA 90041

Four returns ⟶

Dear Mr. Poppa,

Two returns ⟶

    Find enclosed a cassette tape and lyric sheet of the song "Next" for consideration by the Mahalos for their Epic Records debut, which they will begin recording next month. Publishing is available.
    Thank you in advance for your consideration.

Two returns ⟶

Sincerely,

Four returns ⟶

Your name ⟶

A. Writer

SAMPLE LETTER FOR A MANAGER

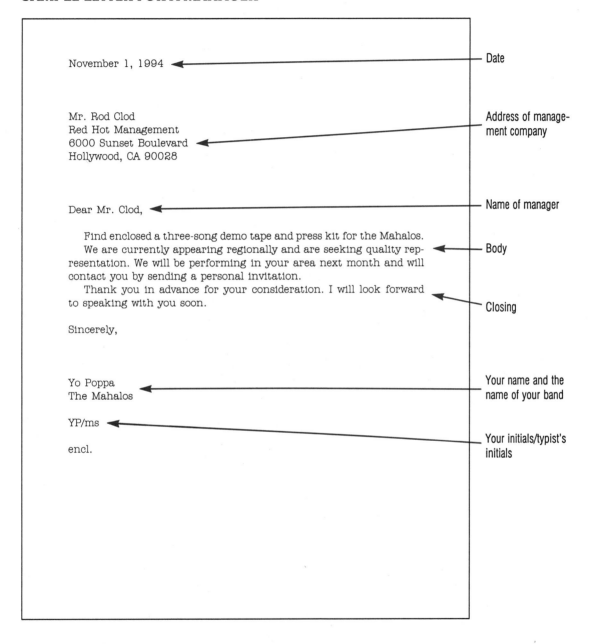

November 1, 1994   ←———— Date

Mr. Rod Clod
Red Hot Management
6000 Sunset Boulevard ←———— Address of management company
Hollywood, CA 90028

Dear Mr. Clod, ←———— Name of manager

    Find enclosed a three-song demo tape and press kit for the Mahalos.
We are currently appearing regionally and are seeking quality rep-←———— Body
resentation. We will be performing in your area next month and will
contact you by sending a personal invitation.
    Thank you in advance for your consideration. I will look forward
to speaking with you soon. ←———— Closing

Sincerely,

Yo Poppa ←———— Your name and the name of your band
The Mahalos

YP/ms ←———— Your initials/typist's initials

encl.

SAMPLE LETTER FOR AGENTS

November 11, 1994

Ms. Joan Nishimoto
Pacific-Asian Artists, Inc.
3390 San Marino St.
Los Angeles, CA 90006

Name of agent

Dear Ms. Nishimoto,

Mention performances in agent's area

Find enclosed a videotape, photos and a press kit for the band, the Mahalos.

The band will be performing a series of shows in your area next month, and we would like to invite you to attend. We will be sending you a list of performances and RSVP information.

Cite enclosures

We have enclosed a list of recent performances in the southern California area in the last year; we are interested in expanding our audience. We are very familiar with the acts that your company is currently representing, and we would like to discuss with you the possibility of being represented by your organization.

State intent to contact

Thank you in advance for your consideration, Ms. Nishimoto. We will contact you within the next week.

Sincerely,

Yo Poppa
The Mahalos

YP/ms

encl.

CHAPTER 5

RECORD COMPANIES

Contrary to what purists would like to believe, the first priority of a record company is to make money, not music. While music industry executives are fond of saying "the music comes first," the reality is that, without profit, the commercial music business couldn't exist.

In order to make a profit, record companies produce the mechanical products of the music business: records, cassettes, CDs and music videos. It sounds simple, but in reality, it's a complicated process: Artist signings and development, song selection, record production, video production, record and video promotion, manufacturing and distribution all fall under the umbrella of "producing mechanical products."

WHAT YOU SHOULD KNOW

Since record labels suffer substantial losses if their products don't sell, they've become extremely selective both with the recording artists they sign and the songs recorded and released. Every time an untested artist is added to their roster, they're gambling with production budgets of several thousands of dollars.

Much of the burden falls on A&R executives, who are responsible for finding, signing and developing new talent as well as finding outside material or helping an artist/writer polish his or her original material. Since the entire process has become so expensive, A&R tends to give more attention to a "complete package"—an artist who writes his own material and has onstage savvy, good looks (especially important in today's video world) and a distinctive voice—someone who is easily marketable. This perfection seldom exists in the real world, but labels continue to look for the best package for the least amount of investment.

The next thing you have to understand is the sheer number of creative, talented individuals who are pursuing the same thing you are. Thousands of singers and songwriters descend daily on the three major U.S. music centers — New York, Los Angeles and Nashville. And though most major record labels and publishers, for legal reasons, don't accept "unsolicited material," their A&R execs *still* have desks piled waist-high (no exaggeration!) with tapes and artist bios.

THE INDIES

The positive side of the story is that you don't need to rely on the major record companies. Small, independent labels (indies) are always looking for new, undiscovered talent — and, because of the proliferation of the entire music industry, there are more outlets to pitch to.

The average record label signs between five and ten new artists each year. Because of the competitive nature of the biz, however, the reality is that if A&R hears an extraordinary talent, they'll sign it in a heartbeat (even if their roster is full and their budget is strained) just to prevent their competition from getting it.

While most singer/songwriters hope for a recording contract with a major label, you will find independent labels are more accessible and open to new talent. Songwriters, especially, should pitch their material to the indies. Singers, however, should be wary of signing with an independent label, especially if it involves a monetary investment. If you see signing with an indie as a step toward getting a major label contract, skip this step and go directly to the major record company. An indie recording contract very seldom attracts major label attention and often works against you.

MAKING CONTACTS

How do you get the record label's attention? By networking, persisting and selling yourself professionally.

The easiest way to get around the "no unsolicited material" barrier is to get to know people in the music business. The industry tends to look at the world in terms of *us* and *them*. That's not to say you can't cross boundaries and become *us* — people do it every day. The key is who you know. Simply put: Friends do business with friends.

If you're a songwriter, your first step should be to join a state or national songwriters' organization like Songwriters' Guild of America (1221 16th Avenue South, Suite 25, Nashville, TN 37203), Nashville Songwriters Association International (NSAI) (1065 16th Avenue South, Suite 25, Nashville, TN 37023) or National Academy of Songwriters (NAS) (6381 Hollywood Blvd. Suite 780, Hollywood, CA 90028). The organizations will educate you, teach you how to protect your interests and provide you with pertinent industry information. For example, most major music meccas have books listing contacts for every area of the music business—publicists, publishers, studios, etc. These books are all well worth their prices. One of the most comprehensive is the *Recording Industry Sourcebook* (3301 Barham Blvd., Suite 300, Los Angeles, CA 90068); it retails for about $60.

Attend all the regional and national conferences you can. Not only will you learn more about what's required professionally, but you'll also be able to rub elbows with industry executives. "Schmoozing" is what the music industry is built on. The more contacts you have, the easier it is to get your song or your promo package into the right hands.

This may sound obvious, but bring plenty of business cards with you to these events; it's so much classier than tearing off strips of paper or writing your number on a cocktail napkin they'll throw away. Use simple, straightforward cards with your name, address and phone number. If you want to add a line with your occupation, opt for "artist/writer" or "writer." A word of caution: Don't be too eager. A&R execs are gun shy and prefer not to have tapes shoved at them over the hors d'oeuvres table. Timing is crucial, so learn the rhythm of the industry before you make any fast moves.

THE PROMOTIONAL PACKAGE

Once you've made the contacts, your next step is putting together a promotional package. If you hope to become a recording artist, this involves a photograph, a biography and demo tape; if you're a songwriter, you'll need a good demo tape plus lyrics.

The Photograph

First the photograph. This is the first impression you'll make, so put some thought into what kind of image you want to project and make sure it's one you're comfortable with. Don't copy someone else's image. Record companies look for creativity, not clones.

Spend some time looking at press photos of recording artists. Notice most are "head shots" (shot from chest-level up) and are not overly dramatic. A front head shot is preferred (although a 45-degree angle is acceptable). Avoid silhouettes, heavily shaded or shadowed poses, and leave the hat at home. Steer clear of "artsy" finishes and beware of glamour shots—A&R execs want to see what you look like; they don't like surprises. It's very important to understand that there are rules for people who are seeking deals that don't apply to people who already have them (for example, it's all right for Hank Williams Jr. to wear a hat in his publicity shot, but it's not all right for you).

Hire a professional entertainment photographer who understands the kind of shot you're looking for. If you don't have one in your area, make arrangements to have a photo shoot when you're in a city that does have one or prepare to be very specific with your local photographer.

Don't put all your money on one or two shots, especially if you're dealing with an inexperienced photographer. Thirty-six shots should be the minimum—double that is better. Then have a contact strip made and pick your proofs (it's a good idea to ask excruciatingly honest friends and relatives for advice). Again, make sure the picture looks like you, not what you want to look like. Once you've selected a pose, have several 8″ × 10″ copies made. Black and white is standard, but color isn't banned as long as the quality is good.

Your name should be imprinted on the bottom margin (centered) of the print. There are businesses that specialize in inexpensive photo reproduction (including having your name imprinted), so don't pay exorbitant rates to have these prints made.

The Bio

The next step is your biography, a condensed version of your life and entertainment career. A&R execs know that if you're just starting out, you're not going to have much of a history, so don't try to "snow" them (i.e., if you once swept the stage after a Willie Nelson concert, don't put "shared the stage with Willie Nelson" in your bio.) A bio shouldn't lie; it's always better to understate than to overstate.

If you find it hard to write about yourself, hire someone experienced in writing artist bios. It is certainly not necessary to hire someone, but professional writers can help you present a professional image. The music industry source books previously mentioned will provide listings of entertainment journalists and publicists you can contact. Depending on what part of the country you live in, having your bios produced will range from $50 to $200 or more. A mid-range price will get you what you need. A professional writer will interview you to get your personal background information and professional history, then incorporate the information succinctly into a *one-page*, single-spaced bio. Don't pay extra for rewrites if you are not satisfied—that's included in the price.

Whether you decide to write the bio yourself or to hire a professional, have your bio professionally printed. Don't just run it through the copy machine. Pick out quality paper stock (white, buff or gray), and be sure to carefully proofread it before you give the final go-ahead. Misspelled words won't create a positive impression.

At the end of this chapter, you will find two models for your bio's text. There is a sample on page 49 of a beginning performer's bio, followed by the text of an early bio that Billy Ray Cyrus actually used (pages 50-51). See chapter seven (page 76) for a sample layout.

The Demo

The last and most important part of your package is your demonstration tape, or demo. Whether pitching to a record label executive, a producer or a music publisher, the rules for the demo are mostly the same.

Writer's Demos. Contrary to what many people may tell you, you don't need to rent a twenty-four-track recording studio and hire a group of professional studio musicians to produce an acceptable product if you are just pitching a song. A well-made, two-track guitar/piano vocal will properly showcase most songs if it meets the minimum standards of the industry. Those standards are a clear sound with no background noise, distortion or tape hiss; a good, sincere vocal performance that gets the meaning of the song across with minimal improvisations and vocal gymnastics; and professional accompaniment that enhances the vocal rather than upstaging it or drowning it out. The exception to this last rule is in cases where the hook of the song you are pitching is based more on the music than the lyric. In this case, choose the instrument that you feel most accurately expresses the mood of your song.

It is also a good rule not to style your demo for one particular artist. If he or she passes on your song, you will have to completely redo your demo to pitch it to another artist. The clone rule for photos also applies to demo vocals—don't use a sound-alike singer. Close is good, but an exact impersonation will usually doom your demo.

There are times when a fully produced demo is better than a two-track instrument/vocal; it's usually a judgment call that only experience can dictate. If you do decide your demo requires what is known in the industry as a "full-blown" demo, here are some tips to help you out:

1. Pick experienced musicians. They may cost you more money than your buddies, but they are faster and have a better sense of what producers and A&R types are looking for. Since most recording studios charge by the hour, you wind up spending about the same but end up with a better product.

2. Less is usually better. Get a good solid rhythm section and one—never more than two—lead instruments.

3. A good sound engineer is a must. Most studios provide one, but before you hire anyone, ask to hear some recent demos; make sure the quality is acceptable. If you don't have any experience in a recording studio, look for a studio that specializes in writers' demos. These studios usually provide musicians and have per-song packages that include excellent engineering for much less than it would cost you to produce a demo yourself. If there are no studios like this in your area, find someone experienced to assist you. The studio can usually help you with this; if not, your local musicians' union can.

Artist's Demos. If you're seeking a recording contract as an artist/writer, the above rules also apply, with some additions and exceptions. Usually, producers and A&R execs want modestly produced (full-blown) demos, but if your voice can be shown in its best light with just a piano/vocal or good guitar/vocal, go for it.

The most important aspect of your demo as an artist is your voice. The photo and bio are nice, but record companies ultimately buy and sell your voice. It must be distinctive (i.e., easily recognizable when heard) and must have a pleasant quality about it that fits the format (e.g., country, rock, rap, classical) you're pursuing. It must also be natural—not affected or, as previously mentioned, a sound-alike. And finally, it must be expressive and sincere. Your voice must sell the listener on the song and the feelings contained therein—this is what A&R execs look for and buy. The rest is just window dressing.

Pay careful attention to material you put on your demo. Your best song should be the first one on the tape. Never save the best for last because it might not be heard. Next, choose songs that showcase your voice and performance ability. If you're a ballad singer, choose your best ballads. If you're a rocker, sing your best up-tempo tunes. And if you don't know what you do best, don't bother pitching to a label until you do. All songs should be originals even if you didn't write them at all; use cover material only if you're pitching yourself as a stylist and have some dynamite arrangements.

The rule in the industry for number of songs (or sides) that you put on the demo is usually not more than four, never more than five; three is best. Let's face it—if you haven't sold them on your voice and singing ability after three songs, they will rarely listen to a fourth or fifth. Again, less is better—it's better to leave them wanting more than to wear their ears out. Put your songs on cassette tapes under thirty minutes long; twenty is ideal (ten minutes per side). Put all your songs on one side—no one bothers to turn a tape over.

Label your tape (custom printed tape labels are best) with your name, address and telephone number. Don't rely on putting the information on the lyric sheets since they regularly get separated from the tape. Then put the tape in a hard plastic case (the soft plastic cases are not as easy to see through).

Always include typed lyric sheets with both writer and artist demos. Check spelling, and don't use correction fluid. The lyric sheets should be folded and attached to the bottom of the box with a rubber band.

HOW TO SUBMIT

Once your package is together, the long process of submissions begins. This is when the contacts you've made through organizations and conferences come in handy. Call your contact at the record label to ask for permission to submit your demo. If your contact isn't in or is unavailable, call back rather than leave a message. That way you don't have to waste your time waiting for a call.

If you want to submit to the label but haven't made a personal contact, perhaps you've worked with a producer who has an "in" with a label and would be willing to submit the package for you. If not, call the label and ask who the A&R director is, then wait a week and call him or her. Don't, under any circumstances, write for permission, since hundreds of letters like this are received and most are returned with a negative reply. When you call, be sure to get the name of the person who reviews the material.

If you're trying for an artist/writer deal, put the head shot, bio and demo tape in a glossy folder (usually available at office supply stores). Don't use the ones schoolchildren use. Paper clip your cover letter to the front and mail it to your contact. Again, make sure the lyrics are folded and securely attached to the bottom of the box with a rubber band.

Either way, put the promotional package in a brightly colored envelope. Plain manila gets lost in the crowd. Address the package to the A&R exec, with "requested material" (although almost everyone now uses this phrase, whether it's requested or not) or "permission given by phone" written on the package. If you're submitting your songs for a specific group or artist, note that on the package as well. Make sure you've got a professional looking package. Custom mailing labels are a nice, inexpensive touch that show you're serious about the business. Type the label—handwriting screams amateur.

Never send a tape or package addressed generically to "A&R Department" and expect it to be taken seriously. There's a good reason record companies only accept requested material—it's because they actually listen to *every* tape that comes in (which is why it sometimes takes weeks for them to get to yours). If they had no restrictions, they'd be overwhelmed by tapes and wouldn't be able to give each one the time and attention it deserves.

The letter (see sample, page 52) that accompanies your tape should be attention-grabbing and should remind the addressee where and when you met (and should be written as soon as possible after the initial meeting). Keep it short and to the point. If you want your tape returned, enclose a self-addressed, stamped envelope; otherwise, it will end up in the recycle bin.

FOLLOWING UP ON SUBMISSIONS

Once you have sent your package, wait a few days (never more than a week), then follow up with a phone call to make sure it arrived at its destination. If it hasn't, ask them to look for it while you wait on the line. If no one can find it, ask for permission to resubmit it. Don't take it personally if no one remembers it or it disappears—it happens with great regularity. If you get a negative response (usually a deadly silence), take heart.

If you're pitching a song, remember that what doesn't work for one artist may work for another or for an album with a different theme. Since the A&R staff and producers listen with tunnel vision for each project, you may have luck resubmitting the song at a different time. Garth Brooks, for example, originally wanted to cut "The River" for his first album, but didn't include it until his third album because that's when "it felt right." Don Schlitz's "The Gambler" was turned down by every major publisher in Nashville several times before Kenny Rogers recorded it and took it to the top of the charts.

IF THEY'RE INTERESTED

If a record label is interested in you as an artist, they'll contact you and either set up a meeting or ask to see you perform live—there really isn't a pattern to signings. Your meeting is just as crucial as your performance. Again, because the marketplace is so competitive, record companies look at the total package. The label decision-makers might as well have "What's in it for me?" tattooed across their foreheads because that's what they're thinking. Be focused and be able to state in a couple of sentences what kind of artist you are. If you don't know, how will you be able to convince anyone else?

In addition to your vocal talent, they'll be checking out your attitude. Are you passionate about your music? How committed are you? Are you available twenty-four hours a day? Willing to put your family life second and dedicate your life to your career? Willing to diet, work out, take voice lessons? If you're not, stop the train and get off now.

A recording contract is much, much more than singing—it's interviewing and doing television and radio appearances, charity benefits and personal appearances on what could be the only two days of the month you're home. It's eating at fine truck stops, sleeping on the bus, listening to hundreds of tapes, then spending days holed up in a recording studio to make your next album so you can begin the interview-and-touring process again. Early in his career, country singer Randy Travis once remarked that all he really wanted was "two days off in a row." There's more day-to-day grind to a recording career than there is glamour, so make sure this is what you really want to do with your life.

If getting a record company deal sounds tough, it's because it is tough, and it doesn't necessarily get easier once you've "made it." Even gospel/pop diva Amy Grant once threatened to quit because "it just wasn't fun anymore." That's when her manager, Dan Harrell, told her, "If it's a hobby, then you stop doing it when it's not fun; if it's something you want to do with your life, then you learn to work hard at it and enjoy it." Or as the old maxim says, "A professional writer (or singer) is simply an amateur who didn't quit."

SAMPLE BIO FOR A BEGINNING PERFORMER

MARY JONES

She's been called "a country Bonnie Raitt," but MARY JONES sings from her own heart. "I dig down deep and let it go," she grins. This feisty red-head captivates audiences with her soulful delivery of bluesy country rhythms. She lives her songs— and she's not afraid to spill her guts on stage so you can live them too.

A native of Apalachicola, Florida, Jones had a natural affinity for music. She began tinkering with the piano at the age of three, taught herself to play "Jesus Loves Me" and, by four, had moved on to duplicating her favorite songs. When the family moved to Orlando, she entered a Christian academy, where she learned to play clarinet. By fifth grade, she was playing first clarinet in the senior high school band. From eighth grade to senior year, she was the school's drum majorette.

Although she had been singing solos in church since age six, Jones got her first taste of show business when school officials brought in a Broadway actress to produce a musical. Mary landed the lead role and toured the Florida panhandle with the production. Buoyed by positive reviews, she decided to pursue a music career.

She won the state-wide Miss Florida Seafood Pageant with her piano/vocal performance, then began singing and playing with an "old time rock and roll" band. In between gigs, she attended beauty school and became a licensed hair stylist. She also started writing songs—country songs. "I've always liked songs that tell a story," she explains, citing Reba McEntire and Tammy Wynette as her early influences.

During a special performance at the Apalachicola Seafood Festival, her throaty vocals caught the attention of Nashville songwriter Robert Smith, who convinced her to come to Music City for an album project. Using some of Nashville's top session players to provide a backdrop for her smokey country blues, she managed to create excitement even among these hardened professionals. Jones can stretch the boundaries of traditional country music to the limit, then reel you back in with a heart-wrenching ballad. "The pickers were excited," she says. "They said the music was really fresh—like Cajun R&B."

But it's the sound of the music that matters, not the labels attached. When MARY JONES pours her soul out in song, people listen. "I sing from my heart," she says. And anyone who has heard her passionate delivery would agree. She's an explosion of high energy emotion gift-wrapped in music. Remember her name—you won't ever forget her voice.

A one-page bio is best for the beginner

Immediately place yourself in your specialty: country, rock, etc.

Quotes add immediacy to a bio

SAMPLE BIO FOR BILLY RAY CYRUS

BILLY RAY CYRUS

Billy Ray Cyrus is a paradox; a quiet, almost tentative Southern Gentleman who "sir's" and "ma'am's" you off-stage but becomes an uninhibited, hip-throbbing dynamo on stage. Raw sex juxtaposed with innocence. It's enough to make you look twice—that is, if you can take your eyes off this well-muscled hunk in the first place.

And *Some Gave All*, his debut Mercury release, is a musical mirror of those contradictions. From the title cut, a poignant personal tribute to Viet Nam vets, to the tongue-in-cheek "I'm So Miserable," to the infinitely danceable, boot-tappin' "Achy Breaky Heart," Billy Ray is a dichotomy of emotion. He growls sexily through a remake of "These Boots Are Made for Walkin'," then switches to a die-hard country two-stepper with "Wher'm I Gonna Live?" before slipping into the heartbreaker, "It Could Have Been Me." His voice is as clear and controlled as his musical emotion is uncontrolled.

How did a preacher's grandson from Flatwoods, Kentucky, learn to sing with such a vengeance? Although he swears he got his start singing a toothless version of "Swing Low, Sweet Chariot" with his father's gospel group, it wasn't until he turned twenty that an "inner voice" told him to get a guitar and begin singing. Sound strange? It did to Billy Ray, too—he'd planned on becoming a professional baseball player. That is, until he gave in, got the guitar and the very next day formed his first band, Sly Dog. Then he set a goal; in ten months, his band would be playing in a bar. "I'd write my goals down," he remembers, "and visualize them. This was my first experiment to see if I could make that goal happen."

One week short of his goal, Sly Dog got its first gig at the Sand Bar in Ironton, Ohio. That's where he first learned what "packing the house" meant. And even though it was a good training ground, even though the audience screamed as the group rocked the place with an eclectic blend of straight-ahead Willie Nelson and Lynyrd Skynyrd, it wasn't enough for Billy Ray Cyrus. He had bigger goals.

When a 1984 fire destroyed the band's equipment, Cyrus took it as a sign to move on. He headed for Los Angeles, assembled another band, then learned to sell cars to support his music habit. "I had to sell cars for a living when I can't even change the oil in my own car," he laughs now, but admits it was depressing at the time. "There I was in Woodland Hills, California, making lots of money but so busy I wasn't having time to pursue my dream."

A letter from his father was the impetus for another career move. "He said, 'Always know where you are and always know where you're going but don't ever forget where you came from.' I felt it was time to get back to my roots, so I moved back to Flatwoods in 1986 to be close to Nashville."

Cyrus spent the next five years headlining five nights a week at the Ragtime Lounge in Huntington, West Virginia, then driving to Music City on his days off. Forty-two times a year, he made the six-hour drive. "I'd get to Nashville on Monday, get in the phone book and call whoever would see me—anybody." Fortunately, one of the people he met was Grand Ole Opry star Del Reeves, who not only listened to Billy Ray's tapes, he cut one of his songs. He also introduced him to his former manager, Jack McFadden, the man who propelled Buck Owens, Keith Whitley, Lorrie Morgan and Merle Haggard to stardom. Within a few months, McFadden agreed to add Cyrus to his roster.

Shortly after, Buddy Cannon, Mercury-Nashville's Manager of A&R, caught Billy Ray's performance with Reba McEntire and Highway 101 at Louisville's Freedom Hall. Later, when label chief Harold Shedd witnessed the hypnotic effect Cyrus had on the crowd in Huntington, West Virginia, he offered Cyrus a recording contract.

Cyrus's LP was co-produced by veterans Joe Scaife and Jim Cotton whose latest credits include K.T. Oslin, the Oak Ridge Boys and Alabama. "Billy Ray is a very unique, spiritual individual," says Scaife. "His album reflects his emotions." Cyrus convinced his producers to use his band, rather than studio musicians, on the album, a move Scaife believes is a vital element of Billy Ray's feeling and sound.

Cyrus also penned six of the album's ten tunes. That's why he packs such a wallop in his performance—he sings from his gut. When he sings hard country, his voice softens and curls around the notes; when he rocks out, it's with an edge. He's not masquerading at that either; he's living both with an intensity that drives his audiences wild.

"I don't do anything matter-of-fact," he confesses. "Most of my songs come to me as fast as I can speak them. The songs on the album that I haven't written are all songs that I relate to. The very best description of my music is my life."

Courtesy of Mercury Nashville, 1992

SAMPLE SUBMISSION LETTER

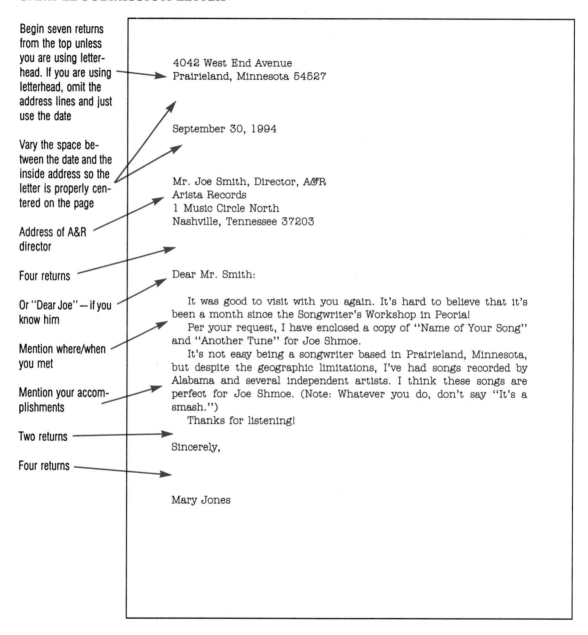

Begin seven returns from the top unless you are using letterhead. If you are using letterhead, omit the address lines and just use the date

Vary the space between the date and the inside address so the letter is properly centered on the page

Address of A&R director

Four returns

Or "Dear Joe" — if you know him

Mention where/when you met

Mention your accomplishments

Two returns

Four returns

4042 West End Avenue
Prairieland, Minnesota 54527

September 30, 1994

Mr. Joe Smith, Director, A&R
Arista Records
1 Music Circle North
Nashville, Tennessee 37203

Dear Mr. Smith:

It was good to visit with you again. It's hard to believe that it's been a month since the Songwriter's Workshop in Peoria!

Per your request, I have enclosed a copy of "Name of Your Song" and "Another Tune" for Joe Shmoe.

It's not easy being a songwriter based in Prairieland, Minnesota, but despite the geographic limitations, I've had songs recorded by Alabama and several independent artists. I think these songs are perfect for Joe Shmoe. (Note: Whatever you do, don't say "It's a smash.")

Thanks for listening!

Sincerely,

Mary Jones

CHAPTER 6

MUSIC PUBLISHERS

The music publisher is supposed to find great songs and bring them to producers and record company A&R representatives in order to get them recorded. To perform these functions, the publisher should be open to working with and developing songwriters and ought to have many connections with possible recording situations.

We are couching this explanation in such skeptical language as "supposed to," "should be" and "ought to" because many people who call themselves music publishers don't perform the traditional publishing functions. Some publishing companies are actually one-man operations who have few or no connections with the mainstream music business and who seem to want to collect copyrights for the sheer number they can accrue. Other publishing companies are multinational conglomerates that behave more like banks than creative entities. A good publisher who will actually work with you and can get recordings of your songs is a very rare find indeed. For suggestions on how to conduct your search, read "Selecting the Proper Publisher" on page 54.

FUNCTION OF A MUSIC PUBLISHER

After the recording on your song has been secured, the publisher functions as the copyright administrator. That means the publisher does all the paperwork involved in securing ownership in and collecting income from the song. If you have not already registered the song with the Copyright Office, the publisher will do that. The publisher issues mechanical licenses—written permissions to record the song that delineate specific payment per record sold. The publisher negotiates and issues synchronization licenses—permission to synchronize the song to film and the amounts to be paid for the use of the song with the film. The publisher arranges for the song to be made into sheet music, usually with another publisher that specializes in print. The publisher collects money from all these sources and then gives you whatever percentage you have agreed to in your contract. The only money that comes directly to you as the songwriter is the performance royalty from ASCAP, BMI or SESAC.

All of the above administrative chores are paperwork, not unlike paperwork in any business. They are not magical rituals. The paperwork can be learned and there are plenty of people who will help at various music business organizations, such as ASCAP, BMI, SESAC and the Harry Fox Agency, an organization that collects mechanical royalties for publishers. The key is to be able to make the connections for your songs. If you can do that, you can be your own publisher and hire a lawyer to do any fancy negotiations that come up. You can even hire a publishing company to do the administrative work (paperwork) for you for a small percentage of the income generated.

However, even some of the most successful writers, who certainly don't need their publishers for credibility, say their publishers are essential to them. For the unestablished songwriter, a publisher is often the only person who will listen and could be instrumental in getting the break you need. Once you have your songwriting foot in the door, you can decide for yourself whether you need to continue with a publisher or have enough clout and connections to do your own songplugging.

If you want to know more about music publishing, read *Music Publishing: A Songwriter's Guide* by Randy Poe (Writer's Digest Books).

SELECTING THE PROPER PUBLISHER

The more accurately you aim your submission, the better your chances something will happen with your song. To make an informed pitch, you need to study the market. Which artists could sing your song and fit its message and feel perfectly? Do they sing outside songs or do they only record their own or their producers' songs? Who published the songs on their latest albums? What record label are they signed to? Does that label have an affiliated publishing company? Who are the hottest publishers around and why are they hot?

Most of this information can be easily found in any issue of *Billboard*, the magazine that covers the music business and publishes charts of the best selling and playing records each week. More information can be found on the record labels. The current *Songwriter's Market* (Writer's Digest Books) contains helpful marketing/submission information about the publishers and producers listed therein. Look for the size and age of the company, the field of music specialty and any recognizable song credits.

Billboard also reports on the movements of music business executives, including publishing personnel. You may want to pursue people who are new on the job because they will be open to new connections.

If, after studying the situation carefully and choosing your target publisher, you are told in no uncertain terms that they do not accept unsolicited tapes, don't give up. Publishers are reacting to a wave of nuisance lawsuits. They need to know that you are not just another lawsuit waiting to happen.

Contact a songwriter organization or performance rights organization and find someone who knows someone at the publishing company you are trying to reach. You may be able to get your tape through a crack in the door if you use a reference from someone the publisher trusts.

WHAT THE MUSIC PUBLISHER WANTS FROM YOU: THE SUBMISSION PACKAGE

Most of all, the music publisher wants a hit song from you and no amount of fancy packaging can make the song on the tape a hit. But few professionals will even listen to your tape if you send it as an unsolicited submission. First, you should get permission by phone to submit a tape. Here is a sample script for your phone conversation:

Publisher: Mega Music

Songwriter: Paula Goodears, please.

Publisher: Who's calling, please?

Songwriter: Wendy Writinhitz

Publisher: Does she know what this is about?

Songwriter: Bob Bender at BMI told me to give Paula a call about showing her some of my songs.

Publisher: Paula does not listen to unsolicited tapes.

Songwriter: Bob said to tell Paula that he recommended me. I've been a member of BMI for many years and he's familiar with my work.

Publisher: All right, you can send the tape.

Songwriter: Shall I put something special on the outside of the envelope so you can distinguish it from an unsolicited tape?

Publisher: Yes, put "Attention: PG"

Songwriter: Thanks a lot. What's your name?

Publisher: Joan.

Songwriter: Thanks, Joan.

Once you have obtained permission, making your tape submission package easy to get into and handle will put the publisher in a receptive mood. A sloppy package will make the publisher want to trash the tape before giving it a listen. So, give your song the best shot it can get by wrapping it in a neat, clean, professional looking submission format.

The Outer Envelope

The first thing the publisher sees is your envelope. Since many publishers are not accepting unsolicited material, what is written on your outer envelope (see sample, page 61) can make the difference between getting it heard and getting it returned unopened. When you make your query phone call to the publisher, as in the sample script above, ask if there is some special notation you should put on the outer envelope. They may give you a specific person's name at the publishing company or a type of song or particular artist they are currently searching for. Examples are "Requested material for Madonna" or "R&B/pop female artist."

Be sure you note the name of the person you speak to in your initial call. Secretaries and assistants are your key for getting through the doors of the decision makers. You might be able to strike up a relationship with the people in the outer office that can lead to a relationship with the executives in the inner offices. Here are a few tips on creating the right look for your envelope:

1. A printed return address looks more professional. If you don't have letterhead stationery and matching envelopes, purchase printed return address labels.
2. Don't be afraid to use colored envelopes. The music business is creative and more informal than some other businesses and professional listeners appreciate the variety.
3. Use a business-size (#10) envelope and secure the flap with a small piece of tape. Don't frustrate the listener by making your package impossible to open by surrounding it with tape.
4. Always send your tape submissions via first-class mail. Registered or certified mail will probably be refused. Weigh your package and affix sufficient postage.

To SASE or Not to SASE

The decision about whether to send a self-addressed, stamped envelope or not is a personal choice. If you do include one, you are giving the publisher the message that you want your tape back, that the publisher will probably reject the song. Even if you do include an SASE and the publisher does reject the song, chances are you will never get a response and your tape will not be returned. In that case, you have lost not only the expense of the tape, but also the cost of the SASE. On the other hand, if you do not include an SASE, there is the slimmest chance that the publisher will pay for the return postage.

If you send an SASE, make sure it is large enough to hold all of the material you want returned and has enough postage on it to cover the return of your entire package. In other words, the SASE should have as much postage on it as the outer envelope does.

The Cover Letter

Keep your cover letter (see sample, page 62) brief and friendly, yet business-like. The music business is more informal than many other businesses. In fact, ultimately the music business is built on personal relationships. If there is some way to briefly make yourself stand out as a person, not just another tape in the pile on the listener's desk, without being obnoxious, do it.

Mention the reason why you are pitching this particular song to this particular publisher at this particular time. This will show the publisher that you have done your homework. Since you have called ahead to get permission to submit the material, include the name of the person you spoke to.

Mention the song title. Include any information that might give the song and you more credibility. Let the publisher know if you or the song have received any recognition, such as winning an award in a songwriting contest. If you are an artist or member of a band, mention that, because more and more publishers want to become involved with the writers who are more than writers. If you have been performing locally to enthusiastic audiences, be sure to tell the publisher. Also, if another artist or band performs the song, briefly state that information and any success related to it, such as "This song was cited as the best crowd pleaser in their set by John Smith, music reviewer for the *Intown Reporter*."

Here are more pointers for developing your cover letter:

1. Use letterhead stationery for a more professional look. If you don't have letterhead, use good quality twenty-pound bond 8½″ × 11″ paper. Do not use erasable paper, paper torn from a notebook or cutesy novelty stationery.
2. Color coordinate your stationery and envelope.
3. Don't tell your life story, but do give pertinent information about your songwriting experience in a few brief sentences.
4. Your cover letter should be no longer than one sheet of paper.
5. Thank the listener for the opportunity to have your song heard.

The Demo Tape

Cassette tapes are the most widely preferred medium for song demos. It is vitally important that you put all your identifying information on the cassette label (see chapter one, page 7 for how this should look). Parts of submission packages often get separated from each other and publishers are left wanting to use songs by songwriters they cannot find. Don't let your cassettes leave home without the following information permanently on the printed label:

1. Song title—does not have to be punctuated
2. Your name or your company name

3. A phone number, complete with area code
4. The copyright notice

Whether or not you send the cassette in its plastic case is your choice. On one hand, it makes the package too bulky to fit into a #10 business envelope; on the other, it can add protection to your tape as well as the chance to include an O-card or J-card.

That's all you need! Popular song publishers are not interested in bios, queries by mail or reply cards. They just want to get into your package fast, pop your cassette tape into their tape decks, be knocked out by the first two lines of your song and have their interest kept up right to the last note.

Use the checklist below so that you don't forget anything before you send off your submissions.

_____ Outer #10 business envelope, flap secured with a two-inch piece of tape

_____ Cover letter, one page

_____ Lyric sheet, see chapter two

_____ Demo cassette tape, without plastic case

_____ SASE #10 with sufficient postage (optional)

Trying to find out what happened to your tape after you sent it is a challenge. You will have to walk a tightrope between being persistent and obnoxious; try not to fall on the latter side. This second call is where your noting the name of the person who answers the phone will come in handy. Just knowing the name and referring to a previous conversation will give you the beginning of a history with this person.

After sending off your tape, wait at least a month before making your follow-up call. Below is a sample script for the follow-up call.

Publisher: Mega Music

Songwriter: May I speak to Paula Goodears?

Publisher: Will she know what this is about?

Songwriter: Is this Joan?

Publisher: Yes. (If it's not Joan, ask for her. You're trying to build a relationship. If she's not available, ask when you should call back; she probably won't call you. If she no longer works there, or if she's not available and you find out that someone else can handle your call just as well, start building a relationship with the new person.)

Songwriter: Hi, Joan. This is Wendy Writinhitz. We spoke about a month ago and I sent a tape to Paula marked "Attention: PG." I'm calling to make sure she received the tape. (If you're dealing with the new person, say: I spoke to Joan last month and she instructed me to send a tape to Paula, etc.)

Publisher: Yes, she has the tape, but she's been out of town and she hasn't had a chance to listen to it.

Songwriter: When do you think she might have the chance?

Publisher: I can't say.

Songwriter: I understand. Well, how about I call back in another couple of weeks? Will she be in town on the week of the 20th?

Publisher: Yes.

Songwriter: Well, thanks a lot, Joan. Talk to you later.

Note: There are some publishers who specialize in developing writer/artists. If you are an artist who records your own songs, it is a good idea to find this kind of publisher. This is another situation entirely and your submission package in this case would be far more extensive. In addition to the basic song submission items listed above, it would include a photo, bio, business card and copies of any favorable articles written about you. For the submission to a publisher who develops writer/artists, follow the instructions in the section in chapter seven entitled "The Record Producer and the Songwriter." For more information on a dual career as a writer/artist, consult *Singing for a Living* by Marta Woodhull (Writer's Digest Books).

PRINT PUBLISHERS

As stated previously, your popular song will not be considered for print publication unless and until it is on the charts. There are other types of songs or musical compositions, however, that go straight from your pen to printed music: band, orchestra and choral pieces. These forms of printed music are sold to schools and churches by publishers who specialize in those markets.

Unlike popular song publishers, choral, religious and educational print music publishers do want to have a fully written arrangement included in your song submission package. This differs from the lead sheet because it contains even more information than you would give a popular song producer. A print music publisher needs to have every note of the arrangement down in black and white. The arrangement must be clear and complete. The best way to do that is to make sure that each part of the arrangement is lined up exactly above or below the other parts that should be sung or played at the same time.

The Choral Arrangement

When submitting a choral piece to a print publisher, you must have a tape of the piece being performed by singers in the age group (grade school, high school, adult) to which the publisher would market the arrangement. This will demonstrate to the publisher that the notes in your arrangement are within the singing range of that age group. In addition, you need to submit the written vocal choral arrangement. It does not have to have the piano part written out.

To find out which print publishers specialize in the type of choral arrangement you have written, do some research at your local sheet music store. Look for material similar to your composition and direct your submissions to that publisher. The sheet music will usually have both the name and address of its publisher on or inside the front page. If only the name is there, the people at the sheet music store can look up the address for you. Your inquiries and submissions should be made to someone on the choral publisher's editorial staff. Call ahead to get a specific name to use in your submission.

You can find a sample handwritten choral arrangement on page 63; your local music store will have examples of printed choral arrangements. A sample choral arrangement cover letter (page 64) and a sample reply card (page 65) are also at the end of this chapter.

Marching Band and Orchestra Arrangements

Instrumental arrangements for high school marching and jazz bands and college or community orchestras have a larger market than most songwriters ever consider. It is an ancillary market that songwriters with composing skills should not overlook.

To find out which publishers deal in the educational sheet music markets, you could ask music teachers about the publishers of the sheet music they use for band and orchestral music. Or you could contact the Music Educator's National Conference (MENC), 1806 Robert Fulton Drive, Reston, Virginia 22091-4348. The phone number is (703) 860-4000. Ask for their publication *Voices of Industry* by Sandy Feldstein, which has a chapter on how to locate and submit to educational sheet music publishers. MENC, a membership organization of music teachers, publishes two magazines, *Music Educators Journal* and *Teaching Music*, in which you can advertise your sheet music for sale.

Submissions to potential print publishers may be made in the same format as submissions of choral arrangements to print publishers. When submitting an arrangement for a marching band, remember that they need the piece to be in 4/4, 2/4 or 6/8 time; it's difficult to waltz down a football field!

All of the instruments must be lined up exactly above or below each other on a full score lead sheet. Do not send the individual pieces of music that each musician reads. Again, the publisher will want to hear a taped performance of the arrangement by your high school band, community orchestra, etc.

The cover letter (see sample, page 66) should be similar to the one used for a choral arrangement submission, with the minor change that instead of a choir, you cite the band or orchestra that performed the piece. The sample on page 67 shows a reply card to include with your letter.

SAMPLE OUTER ENVELOPE

Tania Tunes
1234 Our Street
Hollywood, CA 90028

First Class
Postage for
two or three ounces

Requested material for Aretha Franklin

Peter Publisher
Everyone's Music Company
4321 Your Avenue
New York, NY 10024

SAMPLE COVER LETTER FOR A SONG SUBMISSION TO A PUBLISHER

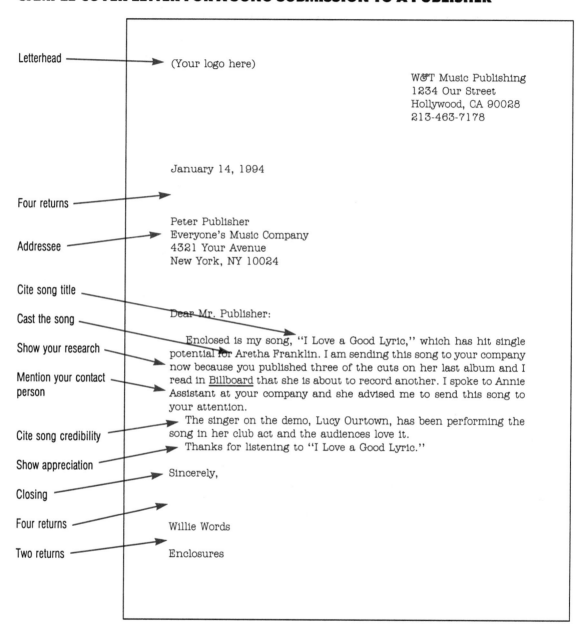

Letterhead

(Your logo here)

W&T Music Publishing
1234 Our Street
Hollywood, CA 90028
213-463-7178

January 14, 1994

Four returns

Addressee

Peter Publisher
Everyone's Music Company
4321 Your Avenue
New York, NY 10024

Cite song title

Cast the song

Show your research

Mention your contact person

Cite song credibility

Show appreciation

Closing

Four returns

Two returns

Dear Mr. Publisher:

Enclosed is my song, "I Love a Good Lyric," which has hit single potential for Aretha Franklin. I am sending this song to your company now because you published three of the cuts on her last album and I read in Billboard that she is about to record another. I spoke to Annie Assistant at your company and she advised me to send this song to your attention.

The singer on the demo, Lucy Ourtown, has been performing the song in her club act and the audiences love it.

Thanks for listening to "I Love a Good Lyric."

Sincerely,

Willie Words

Enclosures

SAMPLE HANDWRITTEN CHORAL ARRANGEMENT

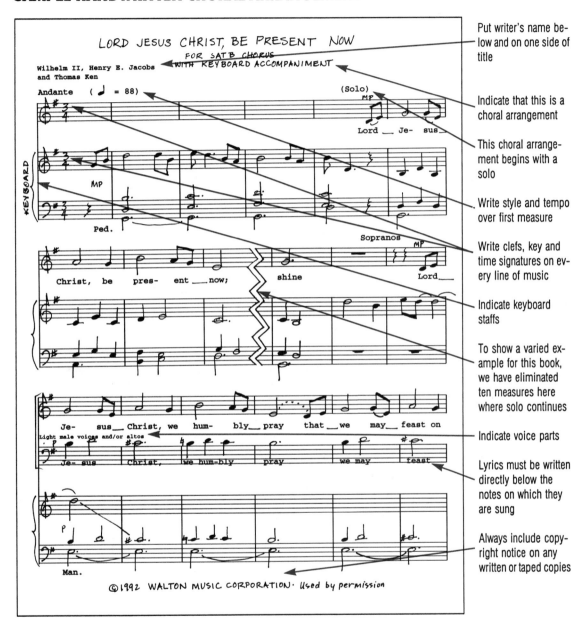

Put writer's name below and on one side of title

Indicate that this is a choral arrangement

This choral arrangement begins with a solo

Write style and tempo over first measure

Write clefs, key and time signatures on every line of music

Indicate keyboard staffs

To show a varied example for this book, we have eliminated ten measures here where solo continues

Indicate voice parts

Lyrics must be written directly below the notes on which they are sung

Always include copyright notice on any written or taped copies

Courtesy of Walton Music, 1992

SAMPLE COVER LETTER FOR A CHORAL ARRANGEMENT SUBMISSION TO A PRINT PUBLISHER

Letterhead

Cathy Choralwriter
999 Singers Lane
Choirville, VA 23435
213-463-7178

June 14, 1994

Mr. Paul Printer
Sacred Sheet Music
7777 Heavenly Ct.
Paradise, CA 90066

Dear Mr. Printer,

Cite title of piece →   Enclosed is a choral piece entitled "Let's Sing Together" for your consideration. The demonstration tape is a recording of the choir of St. Stephen's Church performing the song. The congregation liked it

Cite success with group →   so much that they have chosen to sing it at the end of each Sunday service.

Cite personal credentials →   I have been the choir director at St. Stephen's for ten years and this is the first time the congregation has reacted so positively to a song. I know that your company specializes in publication of this

Demonstrate your research →   kind of choral arrangement because we have enjoyed singing similar compositions that you have published.

Cite other enclosures →   I am also enclosing an arrangement that shows the four-part vocal harmony for the choir. I would appreciate your notifying me that you received this material on the enclosed postcard. I have provided a self-addressed, stamped envelope in which the material can be returned to me, if necessary.

I look forward to hearing from you.

Sincerely,

Cathy Choralwriter

Enclosures

SAMPLE REPLY CARD FOR PRINT PUBLISHERS

stamp

(Front)

Cathy Choralwriter
999 Singers Lane
Choirville, VA 23435

(Back)

We have received your submission of the choral arrangement for ''Let's Sing Together.''

You should hear from us in _____ weeks regarding our decision.

Please sign: _____ and date: _____

Thank you.

SAMPLE COVER LETTER FOR BAND AND ORCHESTRA ARRANGEMENTS

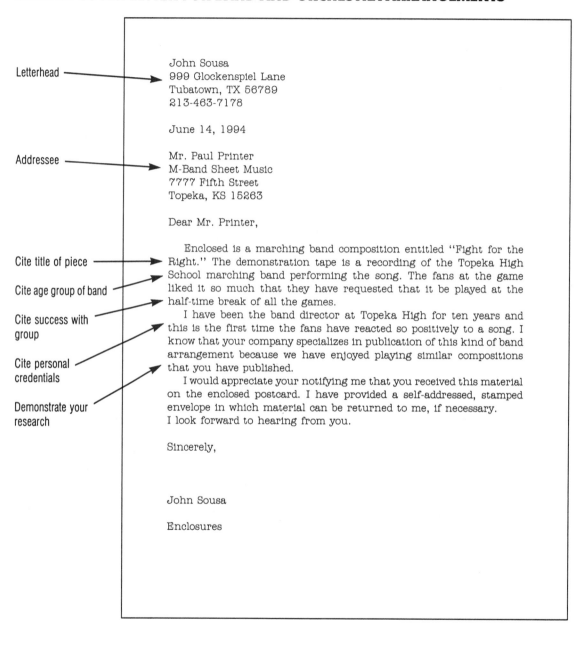

Letterhead

John Sousa
999 Glockenspiel Lane
Tubatown, TX 56789
213-463-7178

June 14, 1994

Addressee

Mr. Paul Printer
M-Band Sheet Music
7777 Fifth Street
Topeka, KS 15263

Dear Mr. Printer,

Cite title of piece

Cite age group of band

Cite success with group

Cite personal credentials

Demonstrate your research

   Enclosed is a marching band composition entitled "Fight for the Right." The demonstration tape is a recording of the Topeka High School marching band performing the song. The fans at the game liked it so much that they have requested that it be played at the half-time break of all the games.
   I have been the band director at Topeka High for ten years and this is the first time the fans have reacted so positively to a song. I know that your company specializes in publication of this kind of band arrangement because we have enjoyed playing similar compositions that you have published.
   I would appreciate your notifying me that you received this material on the enclosed postcard. I have provided a self-addressed, stamped envelope in which material can be returned to me, if necessary.
I look forward to hearing from you.

Sincerely,

John Sousa

Enclosures

SAMPLE REPLY CARD FOR BAND AND ORCHESTRA ARRANGEMENTS

stamp

(Front)

John Sousa
999 Glockenspiel Lane
Tubatown, TX 56789

(Back)

We have received your submission of the marching band arrangement for ''Fight for the Right.''

You should hear from us in _____ weeks regarding our decision.

Please sign: _____ and date: _____

Thank you.

CHAPTER 7

RECORD PRODUCERS

The record producer is to a record what the director is to a motion picture. The record producer has the overall vision of the recording project. The producer is involved in selecting the material and in eliciting the best performance possible from the artist.

What the record producer wants from you is a hit song. He also wants your submission package to be as attractive and easy to access as you can possibly make it. The producer wants to know that you are a proven, professional writer or writer/artist. Producers rely on publishers to do song screening for them. They are not in the business of developing writers. The material has to be there already.

MAKING CONTACT

If the producer does not know you personally, you will probably not be able to get a song through his protective barrier. You will need to establish some credibility in order to get your tape heard. A reference from a music business attorney, a manager, a person at a performance rights organization or another artist he works with will help you to get through to a producer.

The process of making personal contacts in the music business is called networking. The more people you know, the better are your chances that one of them will know the person you want to get to know. The music business is very much a person-to-person business. If you do not live in a major music center, your ability to network may be limited, but it is not eliminated. There are clubs where music is performed, recording studios and radio stations in most medium-sized cities, and these are good places to start meeting people. If you can build a "buzz" (excitement about your songs/band/performances) in your hometown, you can use it as a foundation to make connections in the big music cities.

If you're still working a day job, time your vacation to coincide with one of the major music conventions in Nashville, New York or Los Angeles. The premier event for songwriters is the Songwriters Expo, produced by the Los Angeles Songwriters Showcase, held annually in the fall. At the Expo, over a thousand songwriters come together for a weekend of nonstop learning and connections. There are also similar, though not as large, gatherings for new age music, Latin music, new music and country music. Keep in touch with your local and national songwriter organizations to be informed of these gatherings as they occur. A list of organizations and songwriter's workshops (another good networking opportunity) is printed in the back sections of *Songwriter's Market*.

Unless you are knowledgeable about the kinds of deals that can be made, we recommend that you hire a lawyer to make the deal for you when a producer expresses serious interest. You do not have to have a lawyer already in place to say to the interested producer, "My lawyer makes all my deals. I'll have him/her get in touch with you."

Your local divorce lawyer will not be able to handle this job for you. You will have to hire an attorney who specializes in the music business. The National Academy of Songwriters (NAS) has a panel of attorneys they recommend who offer discounted rates to NAS members. If you are a member of a performance rights organization (ASCAP, BMI or SESAC), they can help you find a reputable music business attorney. Bar associations are another source.

Once you have made the connection and the song is recorded, you can contract with a publisher to do the administration (paperwork) on the song for less than 50 percent.

THE RECORD PRODUCER AND THE SONGWRITER

Producers do not look for songs in general. They look for songs for particular projects during a specific time period as they are preparing to do an album. To find out who is producing a particular artist, look for his name on the album. *Billboard* lists the producers and publishers for the songs on their various charts. Artists do change their producers, so it is a good idea to make sure the same producer will be working on the next album. Record companies have a department called "Artist Relations" and a quick call to that department with the simple question, "Is John Smith still producing Jane Doe" will get you the answer.

Once you have identified the producer you want to contact, call him to find out if he is looking for songs at that time. (See the sample phone script that follows.) You will most likely not talk to the producer personally. Be sure to get the name of the person you talk to. The next time you call, ask for that person by name and mention that you have spoken before. Every little bit helps. Often, the answer is, "No, we don't go into production until next May. Contact us again in March." It will be up to you to keep a tickler system to remind yourself of the appropriate time to call again.

If you wish to submit songs directly to a producer for a project that is about to be recorded, follow the submission package instructions in the section on submitting to music publishers (demo tape, cover letter and lyric sheet). If you go directly to producers with your songs, you are acting as your own publisher. That means that approximately 50 percent of income that would normally go to the publisher for making the contact and administering the copyright will go to you instead.

If you are lucky enough to make a direct connection with a producer, he will probably ask either to be the publisher of the song or to participate in the publishing income. Since most producers are not set up to exploit the song any further than their own recording of it, it is not a good idea to give them all of your publishing income. But since their desire to record is much more certain than a publisher's hope to try to get someone to record, it is worth sharing the publishing income with them.

The Record Producer and the Songwriter/Artist

If your submission to a producer is intended to interest him in producing you as an artist, your package needs to include more information than that of the songwriter pitching a song. You need to include all of the elements in the songwriter's submission package (demo tape, cover letter and lyric sheet) as well as press clippings, a bio and a photograph. The package should be more comprehensive; after all, you're selling more than just a song. The relationship between a producer and an artist is an intimate one, so you will need to convince him that you can work together closely.

Getting Your Foot in the Door

Before sending off your materials, you need to find out how to mark your package or it probably won't get past the receptionist. Below is a sample phone script that could help you make contact:

Producer's Assistant: Hello, Pete Productions

Songwriter: Hi, may I speak to Pete?

Assistant: Who may I say is calling?

Songwriter: I'm Pat Jones of My Tee Music.

Assistant: Will he know what this is about?

Songwriter: Jack Smith at ASCAP told me Pete is selecting material for Janet Jackson's album and recommended that I send him a particular song.

Assistant: We're not accepting unsolicited material for that project.

Songwriter: Jack said he spoke to Pete and this is just the kind of song he's looking for to fill the uptempo gap on the album. Would it help if I had Jack call Pete?

Assistant: That won't be necessary. Just send it along.

Songwriter: How shall I mark the envelope so you won't toss it on the unsolicited pile?

Assistant: Write "Requested material for JJ" on the outside of the envelope.

Songwriter: Thanks a lot. What's your name?

Assistant: Arnold.

Songwriter: Thanks, Arnold. I'll put it in the mail right away.

THE SUBMISSION PACKAGE

The Cover Letter

Your cover letter (see sample, page 74) should explain why you have chosen to approach this particular producer. Did he produce a band that creates music similar to yours? Are you a big fan of his? Why?

You will also have to give concrete evidence that you are serious; that you have been working at this for a while and you are not about to give up. A very brief history of your career or your band's career can be part of your cover letter, with a referral to further information in your bio.

If you or your band are performing regularly or on specific dates you can cite, invite the producer to come and see you. Include free tickets or make sure he knows his name will be at the door so he can get in for free. We heard of one group who supplied airfare for a producer from Los Angeles to fly to Chicago and see them perform.

The Photograph

The producer will want to see what you look like. A good quality 8″ × 10″ black-and-white glossy photograph of you or your band should be part of your submission package. This photograph is an important calling card and worth the investment in a professional photographer who will capture your "image." Producers are looking for something special and new. It's up to you to see that your uniqueness gets expressed by your publicity shot. The photograph on page 75 shows Carrie Newcomer, a writer/artist of thoughtful, intimate songs. Her photograph tells you she is an acoustic artist, and that she's introspective and warm. Make a conscious decision about what you want your photograph to say about you.

For more on your writer/artist press kit, read *Singing for a Living* by Marta Woodhull (Writer's Digest Books).

The Demonstration Tape or Self-Produced Recording

Your demonstration tape (demo) should be on cassette and include your three very best songs. When you are approaching a producer, your demo needs to be a high quality, multitrack studio production. If your group has a self-produced album on cassette or CD, that is even better. Be sure to let the producer know if you already have a track record of sales on your self-produced recording.

The Bio

Your bio tells the producer what you have accomplished so far in your career. Any relevant experience or education can be included. List recordings you have released, if any. If you have had songs recorded by other artists, mention them. List special performances, such as opening for recognizable bands, and name any clubs where you have performed. If you have performed for years and years and the list would be endless, cite an approximate number of clubs and name a few of the most important ones.

Keep your bio to one page if you can. Producers will appreciate seeing a well-organized one-page bio much more than ten pages of meaningless lists. Your bio is an important sales document for your career as an artist. It would be worth it to have this document created on a computer and saved to disk so you can update it and choose stylish fonts. Then you can take the disk to a service or friend who has a laser printer and give it a professional look.

The sample bio and press reviews on pages 76-78 provide variations on how you can present yourself to a producer.

FOLLOWING UP ON SUBMISSIONS

Never give up. Continue to call the producer until he or she has listened to your tape. Below are sample scripts for calls to producers:

After the Artist/Writer Pitch: Follow-Up Call to the Producer

    Producer's Assistant: Hello, Pete Productions

    Songwriter: Hi, may I speak to Pete?

    Assistant: Who may I say is calling?

    Songwriter: I'm Pat Jones of My Tee Music. Is this Arnold?

    Assistant: Yes, how can I help you?

    Songwriter: I spoke to you two weeks ago about sending a song for the Janet Jackson project. I'm calling to verify that you received the tape.

    Assistant: I don't have any record of receiving it. (This is a very common reply.)

    Songwriter: No problem, I'll send another copy. Would you keep an eye out for it? It will be in a green envelope and I'll put "Requested material for JJ" on the outside, as you instructed me to do the last time. The song is called "I'm Ready, Willing and Able." Jack Smith at ASCAP talked to Pete about it and said I should send it along to fill the uptempo gap in the project. I'll get it right out and call to make sure you received it.

Assistant: O.K.

Songwriter: Thanks, Arnold, I appreciate your help. Goodbye.

Second Follow-Up Call to the Producer

You should make a second follow-up call a week to ten days after your first call.

Producer's Assistant: Hello, Pete Productions.

Songwriter: Hi, is this Arnold?

Assistant: Yes, how can I help you?

Songwriter: Arnold, I re-sent that tape of "I'm Ready, Willing and Able" for the Janet Jackson project. Just checking to make sure you received it.

Assistant: Yes, we did.

Songwriter: Great, do you know if Pete has had the chance to listen to it?

Assistant: Well, it's in his listening pile, so I'm sure he'll get back to you if he's interested.

Songwriter: Thanks, Arnold. I appreciate your help. Good-bye.

If Arnold had left an opening, you could have said something like, "I'll call back in a couple of weeks to see what's up." But since he didn't, you just thank him and end the conversation. Then, you do call back in a couple of weeks to see if you can get any indication of interest.

If the producer tells you the song wasn't right (in his view) for the project, don't give up. If you have another song that you think would be good to pitch for the project, say something like: "Well, I'd like to send another song I think would also be great for the project." If you get a positive response to this, try, try again!

SAMPLE COVER LETTER FROM SONGWRITER/ARTIST TO PRODUCER

Letterhead

Pat Jones
Defiance
999 Band Blvd.
San Francisco, CA 94999
213-463-7178

June 14, 1994

Addressee

Peter Producer
1234 Sunset Blvd.
Hollywood, CA 90069

Dear Pete:

Cite your professional contact

Our attorney, Melvin Strong, has been in contact with you and has advised us that you have agreed to give a listen to our band.

Demonstrate your research

We've followed your career for years—Iron Fist, Black Rose, Purple Rage—you've produced the bands we love the most. While our band, Defiance, has those groups at its roots, we have taken the music a couple steps beyond.

Cite success with group

Defiance has been performing regularly in clubs and at concerts in the Bay Area for five years. We write all of our own material and our following has grown steadily. The enclosed bio and press clippings

Cite enclosures

will fill you in on the details of our successes as a band. We are a hard working, serious group, but we don't let that get in the way of having a blast at what we're doing.

Mention local appearances and invite the producer

We will be traveling to Los Angeles the week of October 25th. We'll be playing Club Lingerie on Monday, The Troubador on Tuesday, At My Place on Wednesday and the Name Club on Friday and Saturday. Your name will be at the door for every one of our shows.

We look forward to meeting you.

Drop two lines

Sincerely,

Drop four lines

Pat Jones
for Defiance

SAMPLE PHOTOGRAPH OF CARRIE NEWCOMER

Carrie Newcomer

Windchime Promotions
(812) 333-1721

SAMPLE BIO/PHOTO COMBINATION

Having a photo as part of your bio is an alternative to having both a photo and a bio

Your name is one of the most important things to display on your bio sheet

Make sure the design displays contact information prominently

biography

Carrie Newcomer's dynamic songwriting and performances have earned her the praise of critics. *Folk Roots* called her: **"A musician, poet, and performer of surprising depth and disarming humor."** *Dirty Linen* wrote: **"She has a gift of vocal range and is able to blend several styles into her own unique sound . . . with powerful certainty."** *The Boston Patriot Ledger* noted: **"Her songs reflect a perserverance and optimism lost in much folk music today."** These critics are not alone in noticing that Carrie is a bright new light on the acoustic scene today.

Carrie Newcomer

Carrie Newcomer, formerly the lead vocalist and writer for the highly acclaimed folk trio Stone Soup, has emerged dramatically as a solo singer/songwriter. In 1991 she released her first solo recording, *Visions and Dreams*, and it quickly became popular at public, community, college and commercial radio stations across the country. It was named **one of the top ten recordings of the year** by WUMB in Boston and by *The New England Valley Advocate*. In addition, Carrie was named **best new artist of 1991** by KUNC in Colorado and has appeared on CNN's "Travelogue," "All Things Considered," "A Mountain Stage" and at the 1991 Kerrville Folk Festival.

Carrie has toured extensively across the country playing in some of the country's most respected music rooms including: The Bluebird, Passim, The Ark, The Freight & Salvage and The Cherry Tree. She has performed with premier national artists including David Wilcox, John Gorka, Tuck & Patti, Greg Brown, Bill Morrissey, Al Stewart, Richie Havens, The Story, Maura O'Connell, Pierce Pettis, Tom Paxton, Cheryl Wheeler, Jonathan Edwards and Saffire.

Having grown up in the Chicago region of Indiana, Carrie reflects a Midwestern softspoken charm but also has urban influences in her writing. Carrie has written and performed for several theater productions, and her music has been used by the national Headstart program and The San Francisco Council on Aging. In addition to being a musician, she has been an artist, teacher, truckstop waitress, factory worker, and a volunteer in Costa Rica. These experiences have led Carrie to be a songwriter who is direct and self-assured, yet warm and sensitive. Her songs speak of love and loss, divorce and single parenting, and they touch on political and deeply spiritual issues.

Carrie currently lives in Bloomington, Indiana and will be touring in the U.S. in 1993 in support of her new release "Streamline."

Windchime Promotions
P.O. Box 5653
Bloomington, IN 47407
812 • 333 • 1721

SAMPLE REVIEWS

Carrie Newcomer

"Adorable Carrie Newcomer...created quite a stir amongst the industry folk. Unique, deep warm voice and unpredictable material. Her family portrait 'Love like an immigrant' stood out."
– *Nashville Beat, Music Row Magazine*

"Her arrangements are tasteful and appropriate and never overpower that full voice. She has a gift of vocal range and is able to blend several styles into her own unique sound. Her voice can go from whispery tenderness to bluesy/jazzy spunk to powerful certainty...This one is right up there with the "big kids" Highly recommended."
– **Denise Sofranko**, *Dirty Linen Magazine*

"Carrie Newcomer's strong voice projects a polished, stylish feel to her original songs. An admirable first solo album adorned with a few near gemstones." – *Acoustic Performer*

"This lady is going places...a lady definately worth checking out!" – *Citizen-Times*, Asheville NC

"Carrie has the knack for expressing those often unspoken feelings and unshared perceptions with what appears to be instinctive clarity...Perhaps her facility for capturing a subtle human drama in song is the reason she's written music for so many theater productions." – *Folkfare*

"Newcomer creates a feeling that is distinctly her own. I suspect as a singer and songwriter, she will be inspiring many of us for quite some time." – *Sojourners*

"Newcomer's vocal inflections go from a whisper to a roar...Her songs show a perseverance and optimism lost in much of folk music today." – *The Patriot Ledger*, Boston MA

"A voice reminiscent of Maura O'Connell with flashes of Joni Mitchell and Mary-Chapin Carpenter. Her captivating songs are rich with lyrical imagery and disarmingly confessional". (List of the years best finds)
– **Lynne Lucas**, Greenville, SC

"This release (Visions and Dreams) has it all: marvelous songwriting, wonderful production, thoughtful instrumentation and beautiful vocals...reflective and mature, with an edge of sassiness and verve...another candidate for the 'urban folk' category a la Shawn Colvin, Patty Larkin and David Wilcox. I just call it damn good stuff." – *The New England Valley Advocate*

"She's a vocalist that has the power to raise goose bumps and a songwriter that commands respect. "
– *The Bloomington Monthly*

"..an impressive range, fluidly moving from a caress to an indictment. This woman who can growl or coo is a triple treat." – *The Indianapolis Star*

"Newcomer's rich lyrical imagery reflects her love for poetry." – *The Palm Beach Post*

SAMPLE ALTERNATIVE LAYOUT — REVIEWS AND MEDIA QUOTES

Reviews and Media Quotes

CARRIE NEWCOMER
317/742-5011

OCTOBER NIGHTS

STONE SOUP
October Nights .... RC 102 (Ld)

This folk record has nothing special to recommend it; nothing special that is, but simple, effective, clean-sounding instrumentation, strong, original songs, intelligent poetic lyrics, a lead singer-songwriter with a rich and versatile voice and often unusual vocal delivery, classy packaging, high recording standards—well, you get the picture. No gimmicks.

Stone Soup consists of Dennis Leas (percussion), Larry Smeyak (acoustic and electric guitars, electric bass and harmonicas) and Carrie Newcomer (vocals, acoustic and classical guitars and dulcimer—she is also the main songwriter of the group).

Carrie Newcomer's work might be described as "Joni Mitchell meets Emily Dickinson." Her lyrics are polished and literary; she displays a fondness for minor keys and slightly off-balance melodies which create a mild off-center sensation in the listener; and her subject matter is often introspective and very personal, almost confessional. The singing "lady poet" persona seems to fit.

Standout cuts: "Winter," which almost makes you feel cold physically; "A Piece Of Truth," which allows Dennis Leas to show off his world music approach, using congas, tabla, marimba, glockenspiel, Gamelean chimes and other assorted instruments; "Jack," an unusually relaxed and humorous number about an alley cat who never loses his cool—recorded live, which gives it a nice bright feel; "All Around The Shoreline," a moody a capella landscape piece where the juxtaposition of Carrie's voice and environmental sounds like crickets chirping is as chilling—and thrilling—as a mysterious loon call over a northern lake and "Iowa," which captures perfectly the spacy, packed-in-cotton-wool sensation that a long drive on top of little sleep can create (the way Carrie uses her voice to suggest the sound of a passing truck, very much like Rickie Lee Jones did on "Last Chance Texaco," is particularly effective).

October Nights is an impressive album. Stone Soup deserves wide recognition, and judging by this album, there is every indication that they will get it.

Silo Records Review

"A strong but subtle voice that haunts in a folk song, caresses in a love ballad, or growls and steams in a blues jam..."
Ball State University Daily News

❝ Carrie has a spark, a spark you perceive almost instantly when you meet her or see her perform. Somehow, you just sense that what she's singing is absolutely true. She has no pretenses and you can feel that... ❞
Indianapolis Woman Magazine

"...whisperingly soft-spoken yet amazingly intense. Carrie Newcomer weaves her glorious blue notes around gentle sentiments and barely audible over-the-barnyard anecdotes."
Steve Morely, The Muncie Star

"Her smooth, evocative and versatile voice is the group's centerpiece... establishing instant audience rapport with her relaxed sense of humor."
Purdue University Student News

"Surprising depth, sometimes disarming, always engaging."
Internationally distributed Folk Roots Magazine

"She's a vocalist that has the power to raise goosebumps, and a songwriter who commands respect."
The Bloomington Monthly

"Soothing and captivating...material is well-written and could reach out and touch anyone."
The Indy Zone, Indianapolis

"Sheer artistry and inventiveness."
Oh, sure! Productions, Iowa City, Iowa

"Newcomer's rich lyrical imagery reflects her love for poetry."
The Palm Beach Post

"...Joni Mitchell meets Emily Dickinson. Her lyrics are polished and literary...her subject matter is often introspective and very personal, almost confessional."
Silo Records

"Terrific! the CD especially..."
Mike Flynn, host of nationally syndicated A Folk Sampler

"...a gift for lyrics and an amazing voice."
Jeff Engel, The Daily Iowan, Iowa State University

a rich and versatile voice... the singing "lady poet" persona seems to fit.

Silo Records

CHAPTER 8

ADVERTISING AND COMMERCIAL MUSIC FIRMS

The world of advertising presents many opportunities and challenges for today's music writer. Understanding how advertising agencies and advertisers work is helpful in developing a strategy for submitting material to them.

Advertising agencies exist to service clients who wish to promote and market their products and services. The agency performs a number of duties, including creative development and placement of media (i.e., radio or TV time, print ads and billboards). More simply put, the agency is responsible for both the message and the medium.

THE MEDIUMS

Agencies that handle broadcast accounts (for example, shopping malls, car dealers, furniture stores, etc.) are prime targets for the music writer. These advertisers are often heavy users of radio, TV and cable in their advertising campaigns. Their commercials often use musical images, more frequently referred to as jingles, or background music to drive their advertising messages home.

Radio has long been a favorite medium among advertisers and their agencies because of its ability to target a specific demographic segment of the population. For example, a motorcycle dealer will most likely have better success advertising Harley-Davidson motorcycles on a rock radio station than on a classical or easy listening station. Conversely, a Mercedes-Benz dealer would opt for an easy listening station over a rock station to more effectively reach its target audience.

TV, while often too expensive for the small advertiser, is also an effective medium. The ability to build an image with audio and video in a TV commercial gives the advertiser a distinct advantage.

Cable television has become increasingly popular in the past decade. While at present there is no way to measure the audience of cable TV, cable presents an affordable alternative to radio and network TV for the advertiser on a limited budget.

One similarity exists between all three of these popular mediums: their need for music. A recent survey shows that nearly 80 percent of all broadcast advertisers use music in their commercials. In fact, it would be difficult to think of a major national advertiser that does not.

HOW THE BUSINESS WORKS

The proliferation of music in commercials has spawned a new industry called "the jingle business." You only need to look in your local Yellow Pages to find a jingle company in your town. They are typically listed under the heading "Commercials/Radio and TV" or "Music Production Studios."

Jingles provide an advertiser with a sound, an image and an identity that, if well done, can be easily remembered by radio listeners or TV watchers. This can accomplish three very important goals for an advertiser. The first is to *generate traffic*, or bring people into the business, whether it is a car dealership or a dry cleaner. Hopefully, those consumers will buy the product or service once they enter the establishment, thereby *increasing sales*. Ultimately, an increase in sales will lead to *increased profits*, which is why the advertiser is in the business in the first place.

While this theory is rather basic, it is important for the music writer to understand the function of music in commercials. If a jingle or piece of instrumental music fails to generate these three important elements—traffic, sales and profits—the music has missed the mark, or the advertiser has not properly exposed the commercial to the public on the medium of choice.

Jingle writing has become an art form of sorts. Jingle writers are commissioned and hired to write effective jingles, not songs. While jingles may in fact become songs ("We've Only Just Begun" was actually a jingle for a bank before it was a popular song by the Carpenters), a jingle is designed first and foremost to produce results. Over the years, jingles have become more sophisticated. In many cases, they sound more song-like today than they did previously. In fact, major advertisers will often commission well-known songwriters to write and produce their jingles. The majority of jingles we hear on radio and TV, however, are produced by or through advertising agencies and jingle production companies.

Large advertising agencies like those in New York, Chicago or Los Angeles often have staff music producers or broadcast production specialists. In agencies where such positions exist, it is important to establish contact with these people, as they will typically control how and where a jingle for one of the agency's clients is produced. In the largest agencies, there may actually be staff writers who will subcontract arrangers and producers to take a musical idea and develop it into a finished jingle. It's also not unusual for an agency person to develop lyrics only, leaving the music writing chores to freelancers.

Keep in mind when dealing with agency producers or writers that people working in advertising tend to move around frequently. There is no guarantee that the person with whom you have established a relationship at an agency will be there six months later. The opportunity for the freelance music writer in large agencies certainly exists, but it is difficult to uncover until the writer has established a successful track record with other major advertising clients.

SUBMISSION

The writer may have better luck approaching the jingle or music production company with which the large agency regularly works. Many agencies that do not employ staff writers, and even those that do, go out-of-house for production of their music. In larger markets such as New York, hundreds of jingle companies exist for the sole purpose of creating and producing jingles for broadcast advertisers. Many use freelance writers on an individual project basis. Whether approaching the advertising agency or the outside production company, your approach should be the same. Here are a few do's and don'ts.

The Query Letter

In the music business, like most businesses, time is money. An advertising agency or production company will greatly appreciate the courtesy of a query letter (see sample, page 87) from you prior to the submission of a demo tape.

Keep it short. Creative directors and producers receive tons of mail from writers, so be considerate and businesslike when sending an introductory letter. Include a reply card (see sample, page 88) in the letter—a self-addressed notecard that the producer can mail back to you when he receives your query letter.

If the recipient of your query uses freelancers, you will most likely receive your reply card back. Make sure you stamp and address the reply card. This makes it that much easier for the card to be returned to you. In fact, place the person's name to whom you sent your query in the upper left hand corner of the reply card so you will know who it is from and will save the recipient the trouble of having to fill out his name and address.

While your reply card need not be a work of art, you might try to print it on a colored stock, as opposed to white, or you might opt for an unusually sized card . . . anything that will help the recipient of your query remember yours above the hundreds of others he has received.

The Demo Tape

Once the card comes back, you have one shot at making an impression with your music. The proliferation of MIDI studios in the basements and bedrooms of thousands of music writers around the world has made the field of jingle writing and producing a crowded one. Unfortunately, many writers confuse technology with talent. Just because a writer has a hot MIDI rig with all the latest bells and whistles does not necessarily mean the music that comes out of this equipment is going to be suitable or attractive to either an agency or production company. It's the carpenter's skills, not the tools, that make or break someone's career in the carpentry business. By the same token, the increased number of writers trying to break through makes the number of submissions an agency or production company receives in today's market almost unmanageable. Therefore, *be different!*

Make certain the demo is appropriate. A creative director or broadcast director at an advertising agency is not interested in the three-minute love song you wrote for your girlfriend or the heavy metal tune you submitted to a record company. Run your music by someone who knows music, preferably a professional musician or composer with experience in commercial or AV music. Your parents may love your tape, but they probably do not accurately reflect the kind of opinion you might get from an advertising pro. The agency or production company wants to know that you are familiar with the form of a jingle. Remember, unlike songwriting, when writing a jingle you have either sixty, thirty or, in some cases, fifteen seconds to make your point.

Keep your tape short; three to five minutes is optimum. And always put your best foot forward. Put the piece of music you are most proud of, the one that truly represents just how good you are, *first* on the tape. Many listeners will never get beyond that first composition when auditioning your tape. If you save the best for last, it may never be heard.

Mix up the styles on your tape. Show the listener you are capable of writing and producing any type of music. The needs for music in advertising are as varied as the products and services the music sells. You'll get a great deal of mileage out of a varied demo tape. For example, if you open with a hot rock piece, follow it up with a classical tune you've written. Contrast between such cuts will impress the listener and demonstrate that you are a versatile writer, able to fill any musical need and adapt to any style or situation.

If, on the other hand, you shine in one particular style, let the person know that up front. Much like the agency or production company that is hired to target market a product or service for their client, you can do the same. If you are a great country music writer, say so (see sample, page 89).

Cassettes are the most widely accepted format for demo tapes. However, you might want to determine if the agency to which you're submitting has DAT capability. While considerably more expensive than conventional cassettes, a DAT will make an impression. A DAT will not only sound superior, but it will also show the person reviewing your tape that you are serious about quality. You are more likely to find DAT capability at the production company than the agency, so you will want to check in advance. Consider adding an extra check-off block on your reply card (see sample, page 90).

If you choose to stick with the conventional cassette format, be certain to use a high bias, chrome or metal formulation tape. The best-written piece of music can sound awful on a second-rate tape. Take pride in the product you are submitting, because it may very well be your one and only chance with a particular agency. For more on demo tapes, see chapter one.

Packaging the Demo

Packaging your tape is of utmost importance. A nice-looking package will attract more attention than a handwritten letter on lined paper with an unlabeled cassette tape. A professional presentation will establish the fact that you are probably professional in your approach to music as well. A poor presentation and a cheap cassette will do little to increase your odds of getting work from the agency or production company.

Always mark your cassette with your name, address and, most importantly, your phone number. Invest in professional-looking cassette labels with this information printed on them. If you want your tape to be returned, always enclose a self-addressed stamped envelope (SASE) for the respondent's convenience. Make sure you send your tape in a padded mailbag to minimize the risk of damage in the mail. The SASE should also be a padded one with adequate return postage. If you don't want your tape returned, and in some respects that's best, mention in the letter that accompanies your tape that there is no need to return the tape. Assuming your reply card came back requesting a demo tape, you should send a letter similar to the one on page 91 with your tape.

By closing your letter with the specific time and day you will follow up on the letter, you will catch the person to whom you are submitting off guard. Although being this precise does not increase your chances of getting through, the person will be more likely to remember you because of the way you wrote your letter.

If you are fortunate enough to have been commissioned by an agency or production company to write a jingle in the past, put some samples of jingles for which you've actually been paid on the demo. Be certain to mention this in your letter (see submission letter mentioning credits, page 92). The fact that you've been paid to write a jingle is important and further increases your credibility with the prospect you're pitching.

Close your letter, as always, with the intent to follow up at a later date. As you move forward with new clients, whether agencies or production companies, change your demo often and make certain you update those people who have responded to your queries.

You may want to send out a short press release (see sample, page 93) that you can generate on your computer. Naturally, it is best to send a release when you have more than one thing to talk about. One jingle assignment is not going to bring you the next Coke assignment. But your prospects will never know how and what you're doing if you don't tell them.

FOLLOWING UP ON SUBMISSIONS

The telephone is the quickest way to follow up on the demo tape you've submitted, but your odds of getting through may be slim compared to your chance of getting through by mail. Most everyone opens their mail; not everyone will return phone calls.

When you do call, be polite and, as always, respect the person's time. If you do get through, say something like "Mr. Producer, I wanted to follow up on a demo tape I sent a few weeks ago. Did you have a chance to listen to it?" If the response is "No," and often times it will be, courteously say "I know you're busy, so why don't I give you a call in about ten days and get your reaction to the tape?" Your prospect will appreciate the fact that you aren't trying to badger him or monopolize his time.

If the answer to your initial question is "Yes, I did listen," your response should be "And how did you like it?" Get ready for what will hopefully be an honest critique of your tape. If your prospect says "I like it," you now have an opening to ask if he or she has any projects pending with which you might be able to help. If nothing is happening at the moment, simply thank the person and let them know you'll stay in touch to keep them apprised of any jingles or other types of projects you write and produce in hopes that you might be of service to them down the road.

Persistence is perhaps the most important part of your demo submission strategy. Know when to back off and when to push. Believe it or not, getting an assignment from an agency or production company is sometimes dumb luck; the proverbial being in the right place at the right time. Getting an assignment because you just happened to call at the exact moment something was needed is not uncommon. However, once you get up to bat, your music will have to do the talking.

SUBMITTING DEMOS FOR SPECIFIC PROJECTS

Many music writers feel they have written the ultimate jingle for a major client. How many times have you thought, "If only Coke or McDonald's could hear this concept, they'd buy it for sure." Truth is, it is virtually impossible to get an audience for a jingle you have already written for a specific advertiser. Let's say, for example, you have a great idea for Coke and you do a little research to find out the name of Coca-Cola's advertising agency. (This information is readily available in the *Standard Directory of Advertisers*, which you can find in many local libraries). If you send your tape containing your jingle idea for Coke to the agency, it will be returned to you unopened. Why?

Unsolicited submissions are a no-no in the jingle business, and the reason is simple. Let's say someone actually does listen to your tape at the agency. They return your tape to you, thanking you for your submission and informing you that the concept is inappropriate for Coke at this time. If at some later date, this agency creates a jingle or advertising campaign that even remotely resembles the idea you submitted, you could have a case against that agency. That's the legal reason.

Also, advertisers like Coca-Cola pay their advertising agencies and production companies millions of dollars to develop and test-market campaigns, slogans, jingles, etc. How could someone from the outside possibly have any knowledge of the types of marketing strategies and directions being developed for the client? The bottom line is that you will look like an amateur if you submit a jingle to an agency or production company. You may potentially decrease the odds that you will receive a real assignment in the future.

If, however, you are convinced that your idea needs to be heard by the agency, play it safe. Write a query letter (see sample, page 94) to the agency (always get the name of the creative director or account supervisor who works on the specific account).

There is an outside chance the agency or production company will have a standard release they can send to you. This release will give you permission to submit your tape, holding the agency or production company not liable for the remuneration for your idea in the future.

MUSIC LIBRARIES

We have focused primarily on the jingle business in this chapter, but there are other opportunities for music writers in the advertising field that should not be overlooked. Remember, every jingle writer in the world wants to write the next McDonald's jingle. There are thousands of local, regional and national radio and TV advertisers who use not only jingles, but instrumental music as well in their commercials.

While much of the background music we hear in commercials is custom written and produced by agencies and production companies, many spots use music found in "music libraries." The music library business is a fast-growing industry that can offer opportunity and rewards for the music writer. The basic difference between a jingle or custom-written piece of music for a radio or TV commercial and a piece of music found in a music library is that the library piece is "canned" as opposed to custom-written. Canned music has been written, produced and usually placed on a CD collection without any particular purpose in mind. The music is then made available to producers of radio and TV commercials, as well as to film, video and audiovisual producers.

There are two types of music libraries: "needledrop" or licensed libraries, and "no-needledrop" or buyout libraries. Needledrop libraries license music to producers based on a rate schedule. Each time the producer uses a piece of music in the library, he must pay a licensing fee to the library. Fees vary depending on the usage; for instance, a library piece played as a theme for the Super Bowl will cost considerably more than a piece of music being licensed for use by a college film making class.

No-needledrop or buyout libraries work differently. Music in a no needledrop library is sold outright to the producer with no licensing necessary. The producer is free to use the music contained in the no-needledrop library as often as he likes without any further fees or charges.

Both needledrop and no-needledrop libraries are constantly in the market for quality production music. Both offer great opportunity to the talented writer who understands how background music can complement all types of productions, whether commercial or film and audiovisual works.

The demo submission process for music libraries is identical to that for jingles and advertising music. You will be able to locate the names and addresses of music libraries in trade magazines such as *MIX*, *AV Video* or *Videography*. There are scores of publications dedicated to the production industry; all are good sources for production music outlets. Much like advertising agencies and production companies, music libraries receive hundreds of submissions every year. Follow the same guidelines in submitting your demos, including the query and the follow-up process.

The world of advertising presents many opportunities to today's music writer. Uncovering them can lead to a rewarding and lucrative career for the writer who develops an organized and professional approach to demo submissions. Good luck!

SAMPLE QUERY LETTER

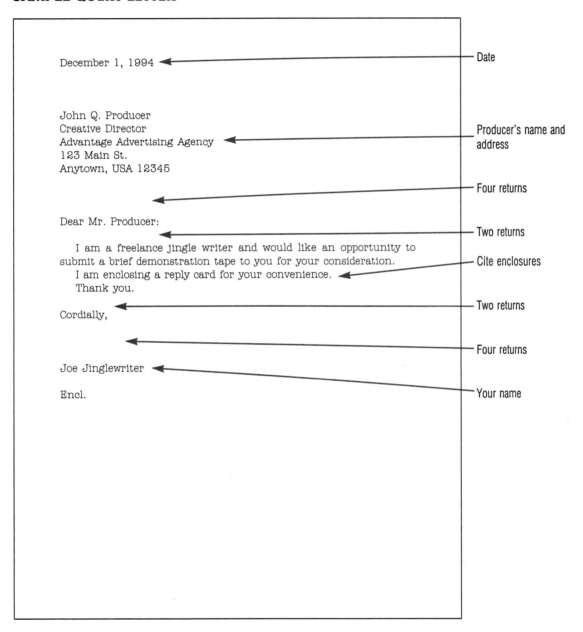

December 1, 1994 — Date

John Q. Producer
Creative Director
Advantage Advertising Agency — Producer's name and address
123 Main St.
Anytown, USA 12345

— Four returns

Dear Mr. Producer: — Two returns

    I am a freelance jingle writer and would like an opportunity to submit a brief demonstration tape to you for your consideration. — Cite enclosures
    I am enclosing a reply card for your convenience.
    Thank you.

Cordially, — Two returns

— Four returns

Joe Jinglewriter — Your name

Encl.

SAMPLE QUERY REPLY CARD

(Front)

From: John Q. Producer
Advantage Advertising Agency   stamp
123 Main St.
Anytown, USA 12345

        Joe Jinglewriter
        321 Central Ave.
        Music City, USA 98765

(Back)

_____ Yes, I'd like to hear your tape.

_____ No, I am not interested at this time.

SAMPLE QUERY LETTER HIGHLIGHTING A SPECIALTY

December 1, 1994

John Q. Producer
Creative Director
Advantage Advertising Agency   ←———— Producer's name and address
123 Main St.
Anytown, USA 12345

Dear Mr. Producer:

    ————— Cite specialty

    I am a freelance jingle writer who specializes in the composition
and production of country music. I would like an opportunity to submit
a brief demonstration tape to you for your consideration.
    I am enclosing a reply card for your convenience. ←———— Cite enclosure
    Thank you.

Cordially,

Joe Jinglewriter ←———— Your name

Encl.

SAMPLE ALTERNATE DAT QUERY REPLY CARD

(Back)

_____ Yes, I'd like to hear your tape.

_____ No, I am not interested at this time.

Please send demo on: _____ cassette _____ DAT

SAMPLE SUBMISSION LETTER

December 6, 1994

John Q. Producer   ← Producer's name and
Creative Director   address
Advantage Advertising Agency
123 Main St.
Anytown, USA 12345

Dear Mr. Producer:

    Thank you for your response to my recent inquiry. As requested,
please find enclosed a brief demonstration cassette of my work.   ← Cite enclosure
    I hope you will enjoy the demo, and I will call you on Wednesday,
April 13 at 4:15 p.m. to speak with you about any upcoming projects   ← Cite specific date and
on which I may be of service.   time you will follow up

Cordially,

Joe Jinglewriter   ← Your name

Encl.

SAMPLE SUBMISSION LETTER MENTIONING CREDITS

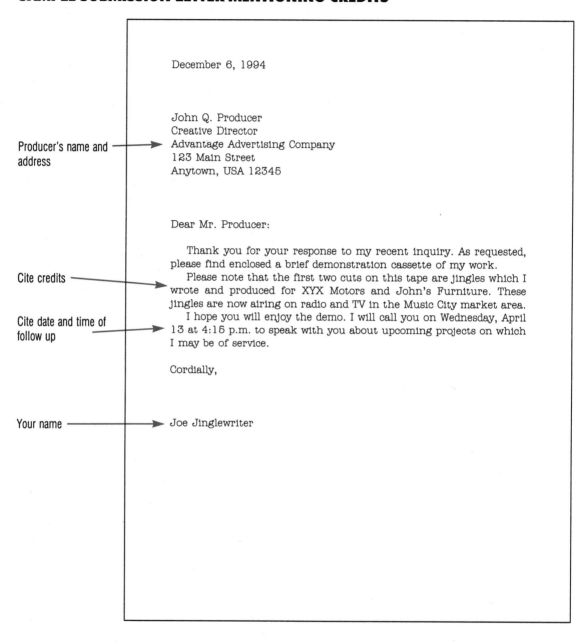

December 6, 1994

Producer's name and address →

John Q. Producer
Creative Director
Advantage Advertising Company
123 Main Street
Anytown, USA 12345

Dear Mr. Producer:

Thank you for your response to my recent inquiry. As requested, please find enclosed a brief demonstration cassette of my work.

Cite credits →

Please note that the first two cuts on this tape are jingles which I wrote and produced for XYX Motors and John's Furniture. These jingles are now airing on radio and TV in the Music City market area.

Cite date and time of follow up →

I hope you will enjoy the demo. I will call you on Wednesday, April 13 at 4:15 p.m. to speak with you about upcoming projects on which I may be of service.

Cordially,

Your name →

Joe Jinglewriter

SAMPLE PRESS RELEASE

Contact: Joe Jinglewriter
(123) 456-7890

FOR IMMEDIATE RELEASE:

ABC Mall, Music City, USA, has chosen Joe Jinglewriter to compose and produce a sixty-second jingle for its upcoming summer radio campaign. The jingle features up-tempo, contemporary sound with mixed vocal chorus and includes the shopping center's new slogan, "Something's Always Happening at ABC Mall!"

Joe Jinglewriter was also commissioned by John Johnson Chrysler/Plymouth to produce a thirty-second jingle for the car dealership's new television spots. The jingle features rock music with a solo lead vocal.

For further information and a demonstration cassette, please return the enclosed reply card.

SAMPLE QUERY LETTER FOR SUBMISSION FOR A SPECIFIC PROJECT

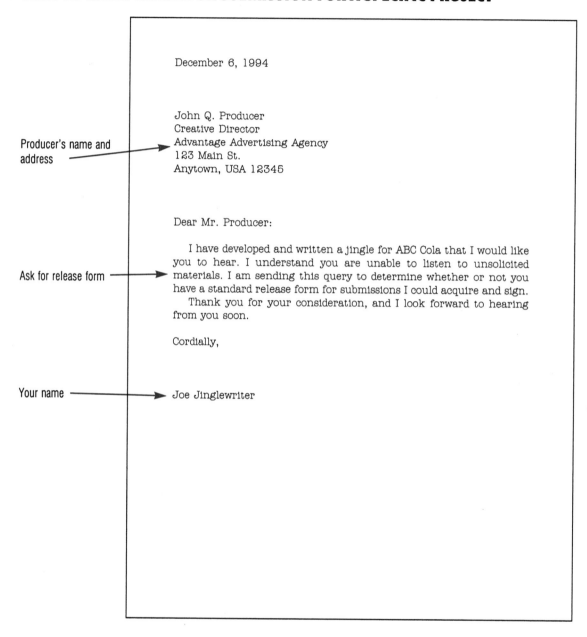

December 6, 1994

Producer's name and address →

John Q. Producer
Creative Director
Advantage Advertising Agency
123 Main St.
Anytown, USA 12345

Dear Mr. Producer:

Ask for release form →

    I have developed and written a jingle for ABC Cola that I would like you to hear. I understand you are unable to listen to unsolicited materials. I am sending this query to determine whether or not you have a standard release form for submissions I could acquire and sign.
    Thank you for your consideration, and I look forward to hearing from you soon.

Cordially,

Your name →

Joe Jinglewriter

CHAPTER 9

PLAY PRODUCERS AND PUBLISHERS

Composers and lyricists seeking to place their work in a challenging and lucrative market should consider writing shows for the musical theater stage. While writing for this form is more difficult than creating pop music, the artistic and financial considerations make it potentially the most gratifying arena available to songwriters.

From an artistic standpoint, writing a musical is both challenging and rewarding. In the course of a show, the composer and lyricist get to present a body of work in a variety of styles. A solidly written musical thus becomes a calling card that shows off a range of your abilities. Producers don't hold a stopwatch on your songs to determine if they're the proper length or fit with this year's hottest sound, so the music is not limited to constraints of radio or contemporary formats.

Financially, there are few creative projects for songwriters as potentially lucrative as a successful musical. Royalties are paid for every performance of every production anywhere in the world. On a hit Broadway show like "The Secret Garden," the composer, lyricist and librettist can each expect to make as much as $7,000 to $10,000 per week from that single production. Multiply that by the number of touring companies, and the figures become even more impressive.

Songwriters make additional money from the original cast album, individual sheet music sales and piano-vocal selections, as well as from royalties from public performances in film, TV or nightclubs. In addition, composer and lyricist share equally in the sale of the property to film or television.

THE THEATER SONGWRITING CRAFT

A musical is a collaboration between three elements: book (also called script or libretto), lyrics and music. All three must work together to create a unified product. Writing music for a stage musical differs from other forms of composing in that the songs constitute only two-thirds of the project. Music and lyrics are judged in the context of the book, and only incidentally as a complete and separate artistic entity.

It is important for each writer on the creative team to understand the work of his collaborators and how their efforts fit together. The book, or libretto, tells a story, sets structure, defines characters and creates appropriate placement for musical numbers. Lyrics serve as an extension of character voice, and must both express the character's mood and match the vocabulary, style and rhythms of the character's dialogue as set by the book. Music dramatizes the lyric and supports the emotions of the dramatic moment.

The most time-efficient way to begin writing a musical is to read the book, develop lyrics based on the characters in the script, and then come up with the music. Composers and lyricists who want to get involved with a project need to find a scriptwriter to work with, preferably a playwright or aspiring film or television writer. The surest route to musical theater disaster is for songwriters to put together a group of songs and then attempt to find a story that fits them. Many failed shows produce cast recordings with great songs that make the project sound like it should have been a winner. In every case, what you can't hear on the album is "book trouble," some failing in the story or structure that caused the show to flop. In musical theater no matter how good your score, if you don't have a strong book, you don't have a show.

Many songwriters think that they can write an entire musical, including the book. We strongly advise against this. Unless you have a strong background in stagecraft, it is not a good idea to attempt to write the libretto as well as the music and lyrics for the musical. Only a small handful of writers in the history of professional theater have successfully accomplished that. Again, the best case scenario is to find a playwright first and plan a show from the ground up that incorporates all the collaborators' desires and vision. The second best way to handle this situation is to locate a play that seems able to lend itself to a musical, gain the rights and work directly with a playwright as the book writer.

Differences Between Pop and Theater Songwriting Craft

Musical theater places greater expectations on your craft than pop songwriting. In all the pop forms, imperfect rhymes are acceptable. Assonance and alliteration rarely appear, except as a substitute for rhyme. By contrast, musical theater producers, publishers and audiences demand the highest level of lyric writing. Ends of lines require perfect rhymes. Internal rhymes are expected. In addition, assonance and alliterations frequently appear to build the word patters within the lyrics. (Study any lyric by Oscar Hammerstein, Cole Porter or Larry Hart to understand the level of craft to which you must aspire.) Lyricists who take liberties with these standards risk having their scores dismissed by those who produce new musicals.

Another difference between theater and pop songwriting is that in pop, the song is complete unto itself, the end product of a moment of "inspiration." That necessity will probably change many times as the script goes through successive drafts, causing you to write multiple songs for the same theatrical moment until you find one that fits. Musicals are not written; they are rewritten, and rewritten, etc. You must be prepared to stick with the evolutionary process of the form and not stop working until you have it right.

LEGALITIES

Collaborators on a musical must have their legal affairs in order before submitting a show. The creators of book, lyrics and music are considered equal partners in the writing of a show and need a collaboration agreement that sets the terms of their working relationship, including what happens to the show elements if the collaboration breaks up. The section on "Joint Works" in *The Songwriter's Guide to Collaboration* by Walter Carte (Writer's Digest Books) offers guidance for drawing up an agreement, and the Dramatists Guild (234 West 44th Street, New York, NY 10036) provides a standard form for use by its members.

If you choose to base your show on pre-existing material not in the public domain, rights must be secured before you develop the show. (The leader of one well-known musical theater workshop used to tell his students to write shows without obtaining rights. He contended that once the finished work was presented to the writer of the original material, rights would happily be granted. His advice proved wrong in a heartbreaking number of cases.) When you finish the writing process, copyright the script and songs (on lead sheets or cassette) as an unpublished collection under a single title. Then you will be ready to begin the submission process.

PREPARING THE SUBMISSION PACKAGE

Wherever you send your show, every submission will require certain standard materials that you must have prepared in advance. Not all of these will be required for every submission, but if you have everything ready you will be able to move quickly when opportunities arise.

Music

Elements for the musical submission include an audiotape, lead sheets and lyric sheets. To avoid hiss and distortion, the audiotape needs to be recorded on high-quality, high-bias tape. The level of production depends upon the sophistication of the recording equipment available to you, your time, your budget, and the needs of the show. In general, musical theater producers prefer a less highly produced recording than pop producers. A piano/vocal recording has been the traditional way to pitch musicals, and many experienced producers still prefer this method, since it allows them to hear the melody clearly. But others like to have a sense of what the orchestrations will sound like, especially if the show features contemporary music.

It's best to choose a middle ground in developing your demo tape. A rule of thumb would be to fill in the picture with some production, but keep your orchestrations conservative. For ballads, try piano/vocal with synthesized strings; for contemporary up-tempo, add the rhythm section. Be careful to avoid overproduction. Your show is better served if you put your time and energies into developing the entire project and not into creating an original cast album.

Take time to find singers who sound like the characters you are creating. Remember that the music always serves the script. The tape of your musical must present characters expressing their deepest thoughts and feelings through the songs. Musical theater singers need to act the moments through their voices rather than simply "put the song across." They must also articulate clearly enough to make words understandable to the thickest of ears.

Record the entire score before submitting the show. If producers prefer an excerpt, choose three to five pieces that best reflect your range of abilities. Make certain your tapes are properly queued and match the script and letter being sent. Label the cassette clearly with the name of the show, the composer and lyricist, and whether the tape contains an excerpt or the complete show (see sample label, page 102).

A J-card (see sample, page 103) is not necessary, but if you plan to use one, include the same information as on the label and add a list of songs, which character performs them, and how to contact the writers. Information about music producer, engineer, instrumentalists and vocalists is not important.

Include lyric sheets for an excerpt submission of your show. Each lyric needs to include your name, address, phone number, the name of the show and all the writers. If a complete script is being submitted, separate lyric sheets are not necessary. While it is a good idea to prepare lead sheets, few producers or publishers are interested in considering them on initial submission. For sample lead sheets, see pages 16-17.

Each of the writing partners need to have current copies of your résumés and biographies available. In addition, if the writers or show have received any publicity, reviews or professional recommendations, they should be included in the submission package.

Libretto
Book materials include a one-page synopsis of the story (see sample, page 104), starting with the premise, briefly spelling out the action and indicating placement of the songs.

The librettist must also prepare bound copies of the script, with title and author credits on the cover. While this format is not as strict as the format for film and television work, the copy is usually centered in the upper third of the page (see sample, page 105). Type size and font are irrelevant, though in these days of computer possibilities, something large, elegant and instantly legible helps announce the arrival of your script.

An inside title page (see sample, page 106) lists the title and author credits as they appear on the cover, plus addresses and phone numbers at the bottom of the page to contact the writers. If an agent represents the work, she should be listed here along with proper contact information.

The second page (see sample, page 107) contains a cast breakdown by age, sex, vocal range and a few important character details, plus an estimation of the number of people required in the chorus to achieve all the roles.

The next page (see sample, page 108) should list musical numbers, who sings them and the page on which the lyrics appear in the script. After the list of musical numbers comes the body of the script.

Queries

It is always best to begin the submission process with a query letter (see sample, page 109) that clearly states the premise and story of your piece, technical requirements, a sense of its style and any development you have done. Most theaters will not consider unsolicited material.

Include the synopsis, a demo tape with three to five songs, and your promotional clips, if any. This makes for a lighter weight, lower postage mailing with enough materials to fairly represent the show, but not enough to make an unreasonable time demand upon the producer or publisher.

To speed response to your query letter, include an SAS postcard (see sample, page 110). Format it with the name of the producer or theater to which you sent the package, a checklist for required materials and a space for a response if they choose to pass on your work. Address this postcard to yourself and clip it on top of the cover letter.

Based on the information checked on your reply card, you will know how to proceed on a full submission.

Submissions

If the theater, producer or publisher responds with interest, promptly send out the requested materials. Your cover letter should acknowledge their submission request, the date it was sent, and list everything you are sending out. The letter should be similar to the sample (page 111). On the outside mailing label, write "Requested Materials Enclosed."

Each submission package should contain a self-addressed stamped envelope (SASE) to guarantee return of materials. In addition, an SAS reply postcard (see sample, page 112) will make it easier for you to keep track of your submissions and how long you need to wait before following up.

THE MARKETS

The two primary markets for musicals are those that produce shows for the stage and those that publish plays. Producing markets include Broadway and off-Broadway, regional theaters, dinner theater and off-off-Broadway. Play publishing covers the children's junior high school and high school markets, churches and stock/amateur. Each has its own definition of what constitutes an acceptable project, and it is important to know which market you are aiming for as you write your show.

PLAY PRODUCERS

Be sure to research theaters and producers for specific submission guidelines. The annual *Writer's Market* (Writer's Digest Books), *Dramatists Sourcebook* (Theater Communications Group) and various publications of the Dramatists Guild provide detailed breakdowns on the submission requirements of theaters around the country. This information will include whether they will accept unsolicited material, if you require an agent or if they will consider your work with the recommendation of a theater professional. It also lists when to submit your material, maximum cast size, technical limitations of the space and how long it will take before you may expect a response.

A typical listing for a theater might be:

> Terrific Theater Company
> Box 123
> Chicago, IL 60666
> Aretha Dwyer, Artistic Director
>
> No unsolicited scripts; synopsis and letter of inquiry, include sample of music and lyrics for musical. We are looking for full-length plays, traditional musicals for the Terrific Theater, 450 seats, proscenium stage, cast limit fifteen; experimental works, paired one-acts, new musicals for the Tiny Terrific, ninety-eight seat black box, no wing or fly space, small cast. Best submission time is December-March. Response in four months for a letter, eight months on a script.

To interpret what needs to be in your submission package and whether this theater is right for your project, you need to take note of the following:

• "No unsolicited scripts" means just that. Send only the materials requested and query the company first. This statement is often followed by a qualifier, such as "Please send query" or "Agent submissions only." Pay close attention to these qualifiers when submitting.

• "Sample of music and lyrics"—your excerpt tape.

• "Traditional musicals"—not interested in experimental works or progressive music for the larger, more commercial space. No hip-hop musicals here.

• "Cast limit fifteen"—includes your chorus. Every actor on stage adds to the production budget, and if your show requires more than the stated number, either trim your cast or skip this submission.

• "Experimental works"—anything that stretches theatrical form, includes unusual themes or musical styles not usually heard on the stage. This is where your hip-hop musical submission belongs.

• "Black box, no wing or fly space"—the theater is an open space with no room to change sets or move them offstage. It requires shows with a single set and limited production requirements.

• "Small cast"—interpretation varies, but usually no more than ten actors, often five or fewer.

• "Best submission time is December-March"—theater seasons run along approximately the same guidelines as the school year. Decisions are usually made on the next season's work by late spring.

By going through listings carefully, you can eliminate all theaters automatically not interested in your musical for reasons of cast size, technical requirements and subject material. Between the listed resource books, you will be able to gather information on all the major producing markets—Broadway, off-Broadway, regional theaters (LORT), dinner theaters, off-off Broadway/ ninety-nine-seat theaters, schools and universities. Aim your submissions at the most likely markets and theaters.

PLAY PUBLISHERS

Play publishers function as agents and promoters for your work in the production markets that generally book one to six performances, usually schools, churches and community theaters. In general, they look for shows meant to be performed for or by children that call for large casts, limited technical requirements and clean material. Playing time of the show is strictly formatted by the age of the audience: children's market, 45-75 minutes; teens, 60-90 minutes; family theater, 90-120 minutes. Music and lyrics tend to require less demanding writing than songs aimed at a Broadway audience.

Play publishers prefer your work to have had at least one production before they will consider it. While many publishers claim to want material relevant to modern kids' lives, most believe that an AIDS-themed musical will not sell. Other elements that can kill your show for this market include offensive, risque or suggestive language or situations; controversial subject matter; and material that is so topical it will be out of date in a few years. On the other hand, if a show fits the requirement of a specific publisher and has had at least one production, the opportunities for publication are excellent.

Publishers place a listing for your show in their catalog, which is mailed out annually to thousands of potential producing entities. Unless a show has received absolutely no response, they plan to keep the scripts listed up to five years and will carry a show indefinitely as long as it is selling. While the royalties in a given year may not be large, on a good show they will be consistent year after year, with no additional expenditure of time or energy on the part of the writers.

Submission procedure remains the same as with play producers. A query consisting of a synopsis, a well-presented audiotape excerpt and clips on you and your partners constitutes your best introductions. After that, it's up to the needs of the publisher and the quality of your work.

SAMPLE CASSETTE LABEL

Be sure to include:

contact information

copyright information

"SHAZAM!" - Excerpts
Music by Ken Composer (818) 555-9270
Lyrics by Lorette Librettist (310) 555-6532

© Copyright 1993 - All rights reserved.

SAMPLE J-CARD

"SHAZAM!"
Music by Ken Composer
Lyrics by Lorette Librettist

Include titles of all
songs on tape

"SHAZAM!"
"Quality Time" - Hank, Marj, Bob, Laura
"Fun, Fun, Fun" - Chorus of Gypsies
"Quiet Eyes" - Hank, Sayna

© Copyright 1995 - All rights reserved.

Ken Composer
10000 North First Street
Burbank, California 91601
(818) 555-9270

Loretta Librettist
123 South First Drive
Beverly Hills, California 90211
(310) 555-6532

SAMPLE SYNOPSIS

Center title ————→

"SHAZAM"
Book and Lyrics by Loretta Librettist
Music by Ken Composer
Synopsis

"Shazam" explores the need for honest communication to ensure the survival of human relationships. It tells the story of a troubled family and the day they spend in a magical world where they are forced to confront their emotions. After a difficult drive filled with bickering ("Quality Time"), the family's car breaks down near a traveling tent show. They are welcomed in ("Here It Is!") by its manager and his Gypsies, who get the family to explore the grounds. At the urging of a cute Gypsy, the daughter, Laura, confronts her teenage anxieties ("Adolescent Blues") and decides to goof off with her new friend. Bill, the son, goes wild in the disco ("Fun, Fun, Fun"), revealing his homosexuality. Gypsies photograph him and bring the photos to Mr. D. Parents Hank and Marj bicker, causing each to go off on their own. Marj faces her loneliness in the House of Mirrors ("My Life") and vows to change. Her bluff is called by Mr. D ("Like My Style?"), who offers her a tempting fling. Meanwhile, Hank has been captivated by Sayna ("You're Wonderful"). At Mr. D's command, the family unwillingly comes together for a Truth Party. When Mr. D. reveals the family's truths, Hank panics ("My Turn!") and runs out with Sanya.

Break between acts ————→

In Act II, the family searches for Hank ("Where Did He Go?"), afraid of the truth they know. Mr. D dismisses them, then renews his advances on Marj ("Like My Style?"). This time, he succeeds. Hank and Sanya share a tender moment ("Quiet Eyes") until interrupted by Laura and her friend. She runs out and Hank runs after her to explain. The Gypsy makes fun of Sanya's feelings for Hank, then dances his success at manipulation ("Fun, Fun Fun" reprise) with the other Gypsies. Alone with the seductive Mr. D, Marj resists condemning her husband for his failings ("When Love Went"). Mr. D gently sends her out to explore more, then gloats over his ease in manipulating people ("Idiots!") and reveals his plan to entrap the family that night. Bob restlessly considers coming out to his family ("Coming out of My Mind") before a Gypsy steers him to the sundown ceremony. Laura avoids Hank and shares her anger with Mr. D, who flirtatiously directs her to the ceremony. Hank and Marj re-meet and

State requirements ————→

Include copyright ————→

awkwardly consider the state of their marriage ("Where Were You?") before the Gypsies take them to the ceremony. The family rejoins the entire camp ("Celebration"), after which Mr. D begins an occult ceremony to trap the family forever. He is stopped by Sanya, who dies as a result. The camp disappears, leaving the family to reconcile with each other based on shared truths ("Quality Time" reprise).

"Shazam" requires a unit set, cast of 3W/3M and minimum chorus of 6.

SAMPLE COVER PAGE

Center copy in upper
third of the page

"SHAZAM!"

Book and Lyrics by Loretta Librettist

Music by Ken Composer

Title

Author credits

SAMPLE TITLE PAGE

"SHAZAM!"

Book and Lyrics by Loretta Librettist

Music by Ken Composer

Loretta Librettist
123 South First Drive
Beverly Hills, CA 90211
(310) 555-6532

Ken Composer
10000 North First Street
Burbank, CA 91601
(818) 555-9270

Ellen Agent
The Ellen Agency
6969 Sunset Blvd., Ste. 1900
Los Angeles, CA 90069
(310) 555-4238

SAMPLE CAST OF CHARACTERS

SHAZAM!
Cast of Characters

HANK—forties, baritone, handsome but shopworn. Man is in mid-life crisis.

MARJ—early forties, soprano, overweight but still attractive. Suffers from a terrible self-image. Hank's wife.

BOB—seventeen, tenor, dancer, attractive and energetic. Gay but hiding it . . . he hopes. Hank and Marj's son.

LAURA—thirteen, alto, a tomboy at adolescence. Hank and Marj's daughter.

MR. D—mature, baritone/bass, charismatic, charming, sexy. A born manipulator.

SAYNA—young, soprano, beautiful, dancer. A quiet presence, thoroughly dominated by Mr. D.

GYPSY CHORUS—minimum three men, three women. Bright, energetic, strong mime and gymnastic. Take on a variety of personas.

SAMPLE LIST OF MUSICAL NUMBERS

For each number include:

1. name of musical number

2. who sings it

3. page on which lyrics appear

SHAZAM!
Musical Numbers

Act I	Performed by	Page
QUALITY TIME	Hank, Marj, Bob, Laura	2
HERE IT IS!	Mr. D, Gypsies	7
ADOLESCENT BLUES	Laura	16
RELATIONSHIPS?	Gypsies, Bob	20
MY LIFE	Marj	29
FUN, FUN, FUN	Gypsies, Bob	33
LIKE MY STYLE?	Mr. D, Marj	38
YOU'RE WONDERFUL	Hank, Sanya	43
MY TURN!	Company	49

Act II		
WHERE DID HE GO?	Marj, Bob, Laura, Mr.D, Gypsies	51
LIKE MY STYLE? — reprise	Mr. D	56
QUIET EYES	Hank, Sanya	59
FUN, FUN, FUN — reprise	Chorus	63
WHERE LOVE WENT	Marj	65
IDIOTS!	Mr. D	71
COMING OUT OF MY MIND	Bob, Hank, Marj, Laura	78
WHERE WERE YOU?	Hank, Marj	83
CELEBRATION!	Company	89
QUALITY TIME — reprise	Hank, Marj, Bob, Laura	96

SAMPLE QUERY LETTER

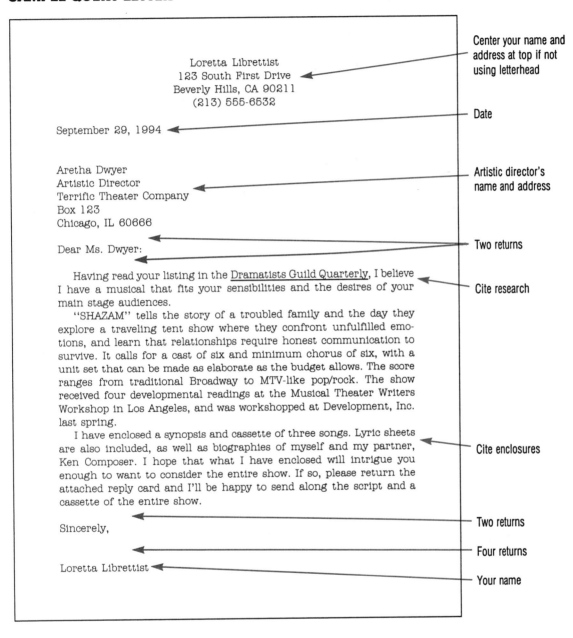

Loretta Librettist
123 South First Drive
Beverly Hills, CA 90211
(213) 555-6532

— Center your name and address at top if not using letterhead

September 29, 1994

— Date

Aretha Dwyer
Artistic Director
Terrific Theater Company
Box 123
Chicago, IL 60666

— Artistic director's name and address

Dear Ms. Dwyer:

— Two returns

Having read your listing in the <u>Dramatists Guild Quarterly</u>, I believe I have a musical that fits your sensibilities and the desires of your main stage audiences.

— Cite research

"SHAZAM" tells the story of a troubled family and the day they explore a traveling tent show where they confront unfulfilled emotions, and learn that relationships require honest communication to survive. It calls for a cast of six and minimum chorus of six, with a unit set that can be made as elaborate as the budget allows. The score ranges from traditional Broadway to MTV-like pop/rock. The show received four developmental readings at the Musical Theater Writers Workshop in Los Angeles, and was workshopped at Development, Inc. last spring.

I have enclosed a synopsis and cassette of three songs. Lyric sheets are also included, as well as biographies of myself and my partner, Ken Composer. I hope that what I have enclosed will intrigue you enough to want to consider the entire show. If so, please return the attached reply card and I'll be happy to send along the script and a cassette of the entire show.

— Cite enclosures

Sincerely,

— Two returns

— Four returns

Loretta Librettist

— Your name

SAMPLE QUERY REPLY POSTCARD

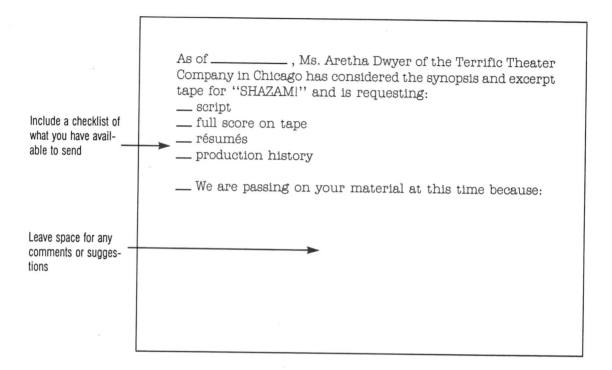

Include a checklist of what you have available to send →

As of _____ , Ms. Aretha Dwyer of the Terrific Theater Company in Chicago has considered the synopsis and excerpt tape for "SHAZAM!" and is requesting:

___ script
___ full score on tape
___ résumés
___ production history

___ We are passing on your material at this time because:

Leave space for any comments or suggestions →

SAMPLE SUBMISSION LETTER

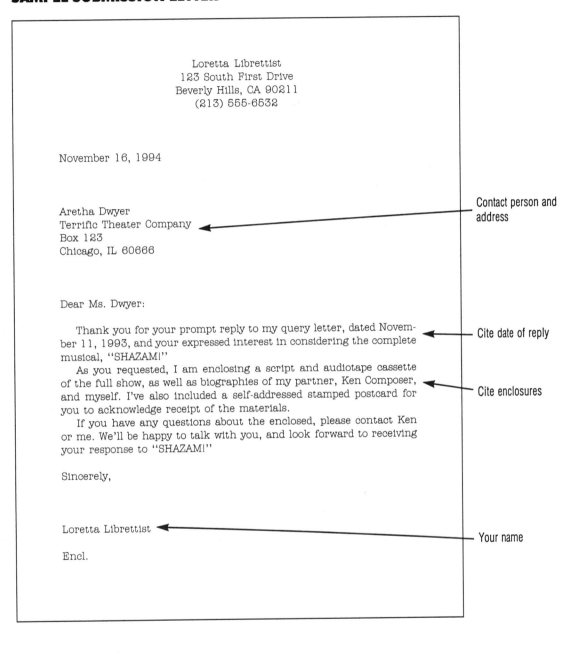

Loretta Librettist
123 South First Drive
Beverly Hills, CA 90211
(213) 555-6532

November 16, 1994

Aretha Dwyer
Terrific Theater Company
Box 123
Chicago, IL 60666

— Contact person and address

Dear Ms. Dwyer:

Thank you for your prompt reply to my query letter, dated November 11, 1993, and your expressed interest in considering the complete musical, "SHAZAM!"

— Cite date of reply

As you requested, I am enclosing a script and audiotape cassette of the full show, as well as biographies of my partner, Ken Composer, and myself. I've also included a self-addressed stamped postcard for you to acknowledge receipt of the materials.

— Cite enclosures

If you have any questions about the enclosed, please contact Ken or me. We'll be happy to talk with you, and look forward to receiving your response to "SHAZAM!"

Sincerely,

Loretta Librettist

— Your name

Encl.

SAMPLE SUBMISSION REPLY CARD

Leave room for a date
so you know when to
follow up

As of _____ , (date) the Musical Theater Company of
Dallas, Texas, has received:
— "Shazam" Script
— "Shazam" Synopsis
— "Shazam" Audiotape
— Resumes
— SASE

You may expect a reply from us within ____ (weeks/
months).

COMMENTS:

CHAPTER 10

FINE ARTS ORGANIZATIONS

Considering the number of opera companies, choral groups and symphony and chamber orchestras in the U.S. today, young composers of classical music face a bewildering set of choices when preparing to submit their material. There are literally thousands of organizations—professional and amateur—from which to choose, which is the good news. The bad news is that not only do composers have to compete among one another for these opportunities, but also with composers who are no longer living. It makes for a pretty crowded field.

But composers should take heart—across the country, interest in and appreciation for classical music is swelling again, and fine arts organizations are incorporating new works into their programming in increasing numbers.

So the opportunities exist. The trick is to target your submissions thoughtfully, present yourself professionally and follow up persistently but courteously. The first step will save you much wasted time, effort and money (to say nothing of the headaches you'll spare the recipients of inappropriate submissions). The second step, as basic as putting your best foot forward, earns you the credibility that will get your submission more than a perfunctory glance. The third step, which is in many ways the most critical, can win you allies in the industry.

TARGETING YOUR SUBMISSIONS

Keep in mind that just because you have chosen not to hire professional management, doesn't mean you should be less committed than a professional would be. If you're serious about getting performances for your compositions, you should apply the same standards to yourself as you would to a professional. Finding the best places to submit requires time and attention. If you treat this aspect of your career as an annoying distraction from the real business of composition, it can ultimately deprive you of opportunities.

There are myriad resources available to composers looking for the right place to send their submissions. Industry directories such as *Musical America*, *Music Industry Directory*, *Sterns Performing Arts Directory*, *Songwriter's Market* and others list fine arts organizations throughout the country, including contact names, annual operating budgets, and in some cases specific information about what the organizations require in their submission packages. Professional service organizations such as the American Symphony Orchestra League, Opera America, Chamber Music America and Chorus America publish annual directories of members that can also be helpful in identifying who's out there.

Narrowing your options is the next step. This involves finding your level of entry. The natural inclination of any artist is to aim high. Having completed your first symphony, you're ready to pack it off to the New York Philharmonic for its U.S. premiere. It's very tempting to imagine that you'll be the composer whose raw talent is plucked from the pile, who doesn't have to engage in the laborious process of working your way up the ladder. But realistically, with limited or no prior performances to your credit, your chances for a performance—even a reading—with such a prestigious organization are next to nothing. As in any profession, you've got to build your experience by starting with the pack at the bottom. Award-winning composer John Corigliano spent more than thirty years working in the business and perfecting his art before reaching the height of his profession. And Verdi wrote other operas before composing La Traviata.

Start locally when seeking out early performance opportunities. Local symphony and chamber orchestras are much more inclined to experiment with new talent, in large part because they don't have to labor under the demands of a subscriber base resistant to new works. Your university or conservatory of music, where you probably already have many personal contacts, is an excellent place to start.

Many times, personal contacts will be the key to getting your work performed. Because of this, membership in professional organizations is important. Don't work in a vacuum. While composition is a solitary art, it's the community you eventually want to reach. Local, regional and national professional service groups will help you learn who's doing what in the field and will help you make contacts and generate interest in the community for your work. For example, say you've composed a string trio in G minor that would require Japanese handbells. A piece with such specific requirements could take years to place with the right chamber orchestra. But through a professional organization, word-of-mouth may connect you with a musician who is interested in just such a work.

Many professional organizations also offer workshops and seminars, performance and recording opportunities, and opportunities to make demo tapes as services to their members. For example, the Minnesota Composers Forum offers reading services through which composers can pay professional musicians to review works in progress. Also, don't overlook membership in area musicians' groups, as they are also good sources for industry contacts.

You can make personal contacts with local orchestras and ensembles by going backstage after performances to greet the conductor and introduce yourself. This establishes an initial contact that can be followed up with a submission by mail. It is not a good idea to follow up by telephone, present the conductor with a submission package on first introduction or monopolize the conductor's time. Make the first contact cordial, but brief and informal.

After identifying a group of local and regional organizations likely to program your work, research them to find out specifically what they program. If travel and budget permit, attend performances to pinpoint just what each conductor is programming and familiarize yourself with the capabilities of the organization. On a mechanical level, is the organization set up to perform the work you've composed? And on a more abstract level, is your work consistent with the type of music being programmed? If the organization is programming more traditional, tonal new works and your piece is stylistically akin to John Cage's 4′33″ (no.2) (O′O″)—in which the composer chopped vegetables in an electric blender and drank the juice for his audience—you would do well to seek out a more progressive conductor. Logically, conductors and music directors are much more interested in giving their time and consideration to composers who've done their homework and are writing the kind of music the organization is interested in programming.

Choosing appropriate outlets for your work may sound exhausting, but consider the alternative. If you omit this step, you could spend a lot more time putting together submission packages that have precious little chance of getting a response. Investing the time and effort in the front end of your submission process saves time and money in the long run. Worse than wasting your time and money, submitting blindly doesn't reflect well on your professionalism. Sure you're hungry for a performance, but if you respect your work enough to make sure you find the right venue for it, you will be taken much more seriously.

THE SUBMISSION PACKAGE

So you've isolated the most probable outlets for your work through research, networking and more research. Next you will need to find out exactly what the organizations you've targeted require in their submission packages. To whom should the package be sent? Because the structure of each organization will be different, it could be the music director, the artistic director, the conductor, a general manager or, in the case of a chamber orchestra, a specific member of the ensemble. What should it include? If a taped performance of the work is required, does the music director want a representative sampling of the work or the whole piece? If a score is required, do they want a conductor's score and parts, or is a reduction preferred? Should program notes be included? If you don't have a performance on tape of the work you want to submit, should you include a tape representative of your ability and style? If you've composed an opera, do you have to have the libretto in hand, or does the company prefer to work with you on its development?

Unfortunately, there are as many different submission package requirements as there are organizations to receive them. It's a dizzying prospect and not very helpful to the composer striving to accommodate all of these preferences. You can find direction by referring to your industry directories, which in most cases list contact names and in some cases list specific submission package requirements. If you can't find details of submission requirements, place a call to your target organization and ask. Sending blind submissions that don't follow procedure put your package at risk of becoming junk mail.

The submission requirements depend a great deal on the composer's individual circumstances, such as experience level, the musical genre of the work to be submitted (symphony, chamber orchestra, opera or choral piece), and the type of organization to which the work is being submitted. In many cases, decisions about submissions are up to the discretion of the composer. But because each package will include four basic elements—cover letter, tape, score and biographical information (or some variation on that theme)—there are some general guidelines that can be useful.

The Cover Letter

In terms of the mechanics of the cover letter (see sample, page 123), the rules of professionalism apply. Use a typeset personal letterhead with a clean but distinctive typeface—Garamond and Helvetica, for example. It's usually a good idea to stick with a simple layout for your letterhead. Trying to distinguish yourself with a flashy layout can distract from the message of the letter itself. If you have a computer with the type font you want and a laser-quality printer (or access to one), go ahead and generate the letterhead and body of the letter on your computer. But if your printer is dot matrix, use a typewriter for the body of the letter. A local quick printer can set up your letterhead at a relatively low cost. Remember, legibility is the most important consideration for both the letterhead and the body of the letter.

Brevity and clarity are essential in your cover letter. State your business up front: You are sending a composition to be considered for performance. If you have been regularly attending performances of the orchestra or opera company, mention it, including the reason you believe your composition is appropriate for the organization—but tread carefully here. It can be a misstep to compare your ability to that of the composers currently programmed, particularly if you're talking about the likes of Strauss and Mozart.

Briefly include specifics about the composition you're submitting: How long is the piece, what is it scored for, special requirements of the piece, whether or not it's been performed before and by whom.

Because composers typically submit the same composition to two or more performing organizations at the same time, it is not necessary to make note of simultaneous submissions in the cover letter. But if the performance of a piece you're submitting would be a premiere, point this out in the cover letter. Also, when the composition is accepted for a premiere, be sure to notify organizations considering it that it has been accepted for performance. Simultaneous submissions are okay, but simultaneous premieres are not. Also, although you should mention if you are submitting for a premiere performance, don't try to sell your piece on this information. Bear in mind that if you're Philip Glass a premiere is a plus, but for most beginning composers it's not a selling point.

If you're submitting your work to a chamber orchestra, alterations to the instrumentation may be necessary. Mention that you are willing to change the piece to fit the structure of that organization. Also, if parts are prepared and available, it would be helpful to include this information.

Conclude your letter by stating you'll follow up within two weeks to make sure the package arrived (see "Follow-Up Procedure" for more information) and sign off. Adding a list of enclosures at the bottom of the letter is also helpful.

The Score

Once again, there are more exceptions than rules that apply to submitting your score. Each organization may have different requirements, and some may not want the score at all. Obviously, you must include the score if you've had no prior performance of the work (and therefore don't have a tape to include). But in some cases, particularly if you're submitting an opera or a very long composition, it is acceptable to include only a tape and indicate in the cover letter that you will forward the score upon request. Also, if you are submitting a vocal work and do not intend to send the score, include a text, lyric sheet or piano reduction. It's another case where the composer is called upon to make a judgment, and having done your homework will help a great deal.

If a score is called for, the conductor's score is most commonly included in submission packages. Never send your original score—remember, much of the material you send out may never come back, and replacing the original is an expensive proposition. A clean, legible copy of the conductor's score reduced to an 8½″ × 11″ photocopy is pretty much industry standard. The legibility rule applies to the score as well as the cover letter. If you've made revisions or other notes on your original score, have a new, final score prepared before photocopying it and sending it out.

If autography isn't your strong suit, either hire a copyist or get a computer-generated final score. There are certain benefits to hiring a copyist for your score. Because they are usually also composers or musicians, they can spot mistakes in the score and work with the composer to correct them. This prevents the errors from being sent on to a music director and becoming production problems. Copyists usually charge by the page, and while there are set union scales, prices can vary. To find a copyist, contact a professional organization or conservatory of music. The American Federation of Musicians (with local chapters across the country) can also connect composers with copyists.

Composers who are serious about integrating computers into the composition process have much research ahead of them. It is an expensive endeavor in terms of time as well as money. For our purposes, it's sufficient to say that music-engraving software programs are available for both IBM and Macintosh applications. Of course, while the cash outlay up front for both hardware and software is considerable, composers who intend to make a profession of writing music will save a great deal on copying expenses in the long run. And in terms of quality, no other method of music notation comes as close to the fineness of traditional plate engraving (which even most publishers have given up due to expense and lack of trained personnel). Lastly, the time invested in learning the software can be recouped later as revisions—which often come before, during and after a first performance—are incorporated into the score in much the same way corrections are made with word processing software. Correcting mistakes line by line as they are discovered saves time and money.

For purposes of the submission package, though, composers should realize that neither computer-generated nor hand-copied scores have a distinct advantage. The greatest advantage a composer can give himself with the score—other than the quality of the music itself—is neatness, cleanliness and legibility. And no matter how you prepare it, proofread your score carefully before mailing it off.

Consider including program notes (if the work is programmatic), an exact instrumentation list and duration of the piece in the score for the conductor's reference. These elements will allow the conductor to see what the piece requires quickly and efficiently. Also, you should note anything unusual about the score that the conductor should be aware of during a reading. For brevity's sake, confine this information to the first inside page of the score, facing the first page of music.

The score should be labeled clearly with the following information on the title page: title of the piece; composer's name; duration of the piece; year it was composed; copyright notice; and, in the case of some vocal works, notice of permission from the copyright holder for use of lyrics or libretto. You should also note who the piece was commissioned by or written for.

Legally, you may include a copyright notice whether or not the copyright has been registered with the Library of Congress. The copyright notice should appear this way: Copyright (or symbol) 1993 by John Q. Composer. The law states that as soon as a composer commits his work to paper, it is copyrighted. However, it is a very good idea to pay the $20 fee and send your score or tape to the Library of Congress to register it. Should a dispute ever arise about the authorship of the work, it falls on the composer to prove he or she wrote the work first. A date of registration with the Library of Congress is the best way to protect yourself.

Some composers send a copy of the score to themselves by registered mail and leave the document unopened, establishing the date of composition with the postmark. Others sell a copy of the score for a token amount to a friend or associate and obtain a dated receipt. These methods may establish proof of ownership, but the best way to protect the long-term rights to your work is by going through the registration procedure. For more information, refer to chapter three. Remember, the date that appears with the copyright notice is the year of registration, not necessarily the year of composition, so if you wrote your work in 1987 and registered it 1990, the latter date will need to appear in the copyright when it is registered.

Composers of opera and vocal works should be aware that if they wish to incorporate lyrics into their work that were not written in collaboration (such as an opera based on J.R.R. Tolkien's *Lord of the Rings* trilogy, or a choral piece set to the poetry of Edna St. Vincent Millay), permission must be granted by the copyright holder before it can be performed. Check the copyright notice in the publication to find out who holds the copyright. Whether the author is living or dead, the publishing company should be able to help you track down the copyright holder for permission. It is wise to determine whether the rights are available before you begin work on the piece—it would be devastating to complete years of work on an opera only to find it cannot be professionally performed, and it has happened.

The Demo Tape
Whether you send a complete piece or a segment of your composition on tape will depend on the specifications of the individual organization. Most prefer to review the work in its entirety, but some may prefer a sample and reserve the right to request more if their interest is piqued by what they hear in the first tape. In any case, you should keep it to one piece per side of a cassette tape if you're submitting more than one work at a time.

Cassette tapes are industry standard for submission of fine arts compositions. Use a high-quality tape (high bias, metal) and cut corners in your budget elsewhere. If the tape breaks or distorts the sound, not only do you undercut your professionalism but your music doesn't get heard.

Ideally, the demo tape serves as an audio introduction to your work and abilities, so make sure the performance is top-notch. If you're submitting only a movement or segment of a piece, choose the portion of the work that best demonstrates your ability. If the only performance tape you have of the work you're submitting is of marginal quality, it's usually better to omit the tape altogether than to send a poor-quality performance in your demo and explain it in the cover letter. It doesn't reflect well on your professionalism to denigrate the performance of others in the business.

If the composition you're submitting has yet to be performed, consider whether it would be appropriate to send a tape of another piece as an example of your work. Once again, it depends on the organization to which you are submitting. If you are submitting to a professional organization—be it an orchestra, opera company or choral group—you can safely assume that the conductor can get from the score everything he needs to know about your piece. To assume otherwise is insulting. You can always indicate in your cover letter that you are willing to forward tapes of other works if the conductor is interested. On the other hand, smaller ensembles and local amateur symphonies may consider it helpful to review other samples of your work. Again, this is a judgment call that depends largely on the level of organization you're submitting to. The better you know the people and organization, the easier it will be to call them. Note: If you do choose to submit a sample tape that is different from the piece you're submitting, clearly indicate this in your cover letter to avoid any confusion.

Your tape should be clearly labeled with the following information: title of the piece; composer's name; the year the composition was written; duration; performers and conductor (e.g., Cincinnati Symphony Orchestra, Jesus Lopez-Cobos, conductor); and copyright notice. Don't forget that, in the case of a taped professional performance, you're also dealing with the rights of the performance organization. Mark your tape "For Perusal Only" to indicate that it is not for broadcast use, unless you have permission to submit it as such. It's also important to remember to credit the performers and conductor on your tape.

Biographical Information

Each submission package should include biographical information (see sample, page 124) about the composer as a personal introduction to the music director. For beginning composers, it is best to use the simple, nonostentatious approach. Summarize your background briefly—one page, double-spaced—including your name, place of birth, where and with whom you studied, degree(s) you received and where you currently live. Mention any awards or recognitions relevant to your career as a composer that you received while studying.

Also briefly sketch the history of your body of work, listing performances either by college ensembles, local orchestras or professional organizations. It's best to work from the top down in this summary. If you've had a performance by the St. Paul Chamber Orchestra, that should appear before the first performance of your work by a smaller organization. You can also list your work chronologically, beginning with the most recent composition and working backward.

If you have media reviews of performances, choose the best and pull a quote or two to highlight the reception of the performance. It is not a good idea to include photocopies of entire reviews in your submission package—remember, brief is best. Also, if you have never had a performance of your work, it is perfectly acceptable to say so.

FOLLOW-UP PROCEDURE

To refer to the process of following up on your submission as a "procedure" is a bit misleading. It implies that composers who follow a prescribed set of steps will achieve a certain result, and there are two problems with that implication: One, there is no prescribed set of steps; and two, there is no guaranteed outcome.

At this time—when your submission package is in the hands of your target performing organization—more than any other, you must depend on your instincts to guide you. Negotiating this phase is tricky because you need to be both persistent and courteous, which can be quite a balancing act.

Your personal contacts in the industry—whether you're in contact with the second violin at your local symphony or acquainted with a baritone in a regional choral group—will help you immeasurably at this stage. They can tip you off to what's happening within the organization in terms of programming, season schedule and future plans.

Personal contacts can also give you the most accurate reading possible on the status of your submission: Has the music director reviewed it? Is he interested? Is he out of town and holding submissions for a few months? Access to this kind of inside information can help you gauge when a phone call might be unwelcome, for example, or when it might be very effective.

To a great extent, your success in following up will depend not only on the extent of your personal contacts but your own sense of diplomacy, tact and timing. Remember, in all likelihood, the music director has heaps of submissions to review. With larger orchestras and opera companies, it can take years to place a composition, so patience is critical. And the worst thing you can do from a public relations standpoint is get yourself labeled a nuisance.

There are ways to tactfully open the door to follow-up contacts. Some composers include self-addressed, stamped reply postcards in their submission packages. These cards can require as little as a checkmark inside a box indicating that the music director has seen the package. They can be useful in the event that the composer does not have a personal contact at the organization.

Placing a phone call to find out whether the package arrived can be effective if the composer has a personal contact in the organization. This call can also open the door for the composer to inquire about when a second follow-up call or letter might be appropriate.

Keeping up-to-date files on your submissions and follow-up contacts is a good way to keep track of multiple and simultaneous submissions. If, for example, you've submitted a piano sonata to three or four area colleges, create a file for the piece and include in it the date of submission and thorough notes dating and detailing each follow-up contact. Two or three weeks later, if you receive your reply postcard back, note it and date it. A month after that, if you place a call to inquire about the status of the submission and the conductor tells you he'll look at it in two weeks and get back to you, do the same. If your sonata is accepted for premiere, refer to your file and notify the other organizations to which you submitted.

Because placing a composition can take a year or more, these files will be your guide to where each submission is within each organization. They will also keep you from following up too frequently, or offending your contact by following up inappropriately. Again, organization in this stage is a reflection of your professionalism.

Many exciting performance opportunities exist for composers today in the world of classical music composition. In this industry, like any other, networking is a critical key. Presenting yourself as a professional will help you become one, and the closer you are to the nucleus of the organization in which you want to perform your work, the better your chances of success.

SAMPLE COVER LETTER

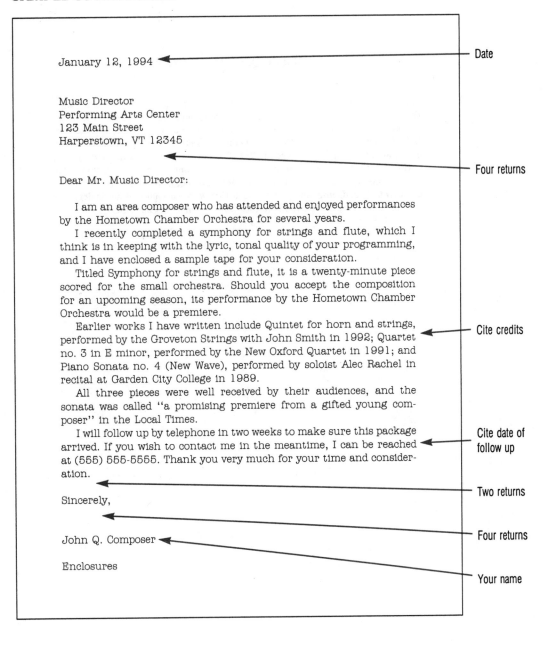

January 12, 1994 ◀───────────────────────── Date

Music Director
Performing Arts Center
123 Main Street
Harperstown, VT 12345

◀───────────────────────── Four returns

Dear Mr. Music Director:

I am an area composer who has attended and enjoyed performances by the Hometown Chamber Orchestra for several years.

I recently completed a symphony for strings and flute, which I think is in keeping with the lyric, tonal quality of your programming, and I have enclosed a sample tape for your consideration.

Titled Symphony for strings and flute, it is a twenty-minute piece scored for the small orchestra. Should you accept the composition for an upcoming season, its performance by the Hometown Chamber Orchestra would be a premiere.

Earlier works I have written include Quintet for horn and strings, performed by the Groveton Strings with John Smith in 1992; Quartet no. 3 in E minor, performed by the New Oxford Quartet in 1991; and Piano Sonata no. 4 (New Wave), performed by soloist Alec Rachel in recital at Garden City College in 1989. ◀──── Cite credits

All three pieces were well received by their audiences, and the sonata was called "a promising premiere from a gifted young composer" in the Local Times.

I will follow up by telephone in two weeks to make sure this package arrived. If you wish to contact me in the meantime, I can be reached at (555) 555-5555. Thank you very much for your time and consideration. ◀──── Cite date of follow up

◀───────────────────────── Two returns

Sincerely,

◀───────────────────────── Four returns

John Q. Composer ◀────

Enclosures

───────── Your name

SAMPLE BIOGRAPHICAL INFORMATION

JOHN Q. COMPOSER

John Q. Composer, 34, has been composing classical music for performance since 1985. Performances of his compositions include Quintet for horn and strings by the Groveton Strings with John Smith in 1992; Quartet no. 3 in E minor by the New Oxford Quartet in 1991; and Piano Sonata no. 4 (New Wave) by soloist Alec Rachel in recital at Garden City College in 1989. The Local Times called the performance of Composer's Piano Sonata no. 4 (New Wave) a "promising premiere from a gifted young composer." A native of Groveton, Ohio, Composer was graduated from Garden City College-Conservatory of Music in 1985 with a bachelor of music degree in composition. Composer currently resides with his family in Garden City.

CHAPTER 11

CONTESTS

Contests provide songwriters, singers and bands with an opportunity for the acknowledgement and validation of their talent as well as an opportunity to win prizes.

Contests are created for many different reasons and it's important to be able to assess whether or not it's a waste of money to submit material at all. Most contests are created to make money, though there are always contests that spring up for other reasons; for example, to find a theme song for an organization or a city. There have been several competitions for a new national anthem, for instance. Many nonprofit songwriting and music organizations use competitions to raise operating funds. These contests are usually open to writers from all over the country.

MAKING CONTACTS

The loftier reason for contests, aside from making money, is to find and expose new talent. Seldom do contests translate directly into commercially successful record deals, hit songs, etc. There are, however, a wide range of potential benefits depending on the scope of the contest.

In the American Song Festival and Music City Song Festivals, each song was heard by several judges, who could turn in the code numbers of songs they particularly liked. After the contest was over, the judges would be provided with a list of the writers each requested and their addresses and phone numbers so they could request additional material on their own. This benefit was a valuable door opener for many writers to establish ongoing relationships with the judges who were music publishers and producers. Although these festivals are no longer in existence, they set a standard for the industry. Many contests today have similar judging procedures that provide songwriters with opportunities to make contacts and gain exposure.

Beyond prizes and validation, one of the valuable benefits was that winners were provided with more door opening tools via the publicity they received as contest winners. This could, in turn, be used for inclusion in query letters to industry professionals requesting permission to send tapes.

SUBMISSION PROCEDURES

Each competition will give you its own submission requirements on the entry blank, but the following are common to all.

The Entry Form

An entry form (see sample, page 132) is included with each song submitted in each category (if there is more than one category). Be sure to fill out each form completely as though it were the only one submitted. In nearly all cases, it is acceptable to make photocopies of the original form. To save yourself some work, fill out the basic name/address/phone information on the original before making the copies so all you have to add is song titles; writer(s), if different; and categories.

The Cassette

Your song has a better chance of staying in the race if your submission package includes a well-produced demo. This doesn't mean spending $500 to $1,000 in a state-of-the-art studio. But it does mean that your singer should be convincing (don't sing it yourself if you're not the best singer for it), the sound should be clean (without distortion and tape hiss) and the tape copy clean.

Songwriting competitions usually require one song per cassette to facilitate easy coding and tracking of a song, eliminate confusion among judges regarding which song is to be heard, and make it easier to re-cue for the next judge.

Many competitions request that your name not appear on the tape or lyric sheet to avoid the possibility of favoritism should the judge recognize the name of a writer. It is especially important, in those cases, for the writer or performer to completely fill out the submission form so that the person initially processing the tape can code the submission form, the lyric sheet and tape. Don't be too concerned about leaving your name off, though. If you don't eliminate your name, the contest will black it out themselves. In fact, it's always a good idea to have a proper copyright notice (year, © copyright owner) on each lyric sheet no matter where you send it or for what purpose. For more information on creating a demo, see chapter one.

The Lyric Sheet

A lyric sheet is usually requested to speed the judging process. A judge can listen to and judge a song by listening to a verse and chorus of the song while scanning the remainder of the lyric. Lyric sheets should always look as professional as possible and be neatly typed with sections separated. Caption the sections "verse," "prechorus" (if applicable), "chorus" and "bridge" and lay them out visually on the lyric sheet so that a judge can immediately "see" the form of your song. You can separate each segment by skipping a line, indenting all the choruses the same amount and double indenting the bridge, or just indenting the bridge and typing the chorus in all uppercase type in contrast to upper- and lowercase for the other sections. This is very important since use of form is a major factor in the success of songs, and consequently one of the factors that will influence a judge. For more information on lyric sheets, see chapter two.

The Fee

A fee is required for each tape submitted in each category. Fees can range up to $15 or more per song per category. Entry fees are certainly justifiable. It is not cheap to promote and organize a contest of any kind. Advertising is expensive and, as the now-defunct American Song Festival discovered, it's not enough just to announce that the deadlines are rolling around and assume that those songwriters who entered last year will automatically enter again. Each year they have to go after a whole new group of writers. Last year's entrants who didn't receive at least an honorable mention are likely to believe that, if someone didn't recognize their hit, the contest is a rip-off and the judges don't know anything. The last thing they'll allow themselves to believe is that their song just wasn't good enough. As a result, they will not re-enter the contest.

In addition to advertising, contests must hire people to process entries, schedule, coordinate and supervise judges and judging sessions, keep financial records, answer phone inquiries and many other tasks. In some cases, judges are also paid.

Some critics have actually advised writers not to pay a fee for submission to contests, particularly if they get a critique because "you should never pay for a critique." Nonsense! (That philosophy originated as a way to protect writers from song sharks who would ask a writer to pay a small fee for a critique, then give the song a rave review as a way to set them up for a publishing contract for which they would ask for an even greater fee.)

CONTEST CATEGORIES

There are great variations between contests when it comes to categories. The major groupings are amateur and professional. Some contests will rightfully place great importance on the division between amateur and professional songwriters with a variety of methods of making the distinction. One method is to disqualify you in the amateur category if you are a member of BMI,

ASCAP or SESAC with the erroneous assumption that, to be a member of a performing rights organization, you must have a song released on record. In reality, though it is impractical to belong if you don't have a record released, the organizations may sign a writer if they feel the writer is talented enough to release one in the near future.

Another method is that used by the *Billboard*/Kentucky Fried Chicken competition in which you can only enter if you have not averaged more than $5,000 per year in songwriting royalties since 1988. This method gives great latitude because one can still be an excellent professional songwriter and not have attained that goal.

Yet another method is that one may not enter the amateur category if they've had a song released on record before a certain date, usually the deadline date. This method has caused great problems, at times requiring notarized affidavits as proof and delaying the final disposition of prizes based on objections of amateur entrants. However, this is still, probably, the fairest way to divide categories.

Your best strategy, if you feel you are an exceptional writer (don't we all?), is not to allow your ego to take you into the professional category. Without breaking any rules, stay in the amateur group if possible.

Stylistic categories, though fairer for obvious reasons, are problematic mostly because songwriters, amateurs in particular, often have difficulty distinguishing pop from r&b or rock, country from folk, etc. They either enter the same songs in several categories just to be safe, or risk entering one song in an inappropriate category and having it eliminated, not because it's not a quality song but because of a poor category choice. The best approach is to play it safe by entering more than one category if you can afford it, but only after getting as much feedback as you can from fellow writers and friends on the most appropriate category.

CHOOSING YOUR BEST SONG

Making the choice of which songs to enter involves a process of elimination, which, in fact, is the process used in judging as well. So it may be instructive to come from the viewpoint of a judge who knows that certain factors will preclude a song from being a winner even though it may receive an honorable mention. The bottom line in most contests is commercial potential, since most contest organizers dream of turning up winning songs that have a good possibility of being recorded by major artists. This makes it much easier to promote the contest next time around, gives it credibility with the music industry and potential music industry judges (who also hope to find a hit), and shows potential entrants that something wonderful can happen to their careers by entering this contest. Because of that bottom line, judges will look at your song in the same way they would judge any song that came across their desk.

Here are a few of the things that may eliminate your songs from the competition, since judges already know that the winning writers won't make these errors:

1. A song without a chorus, unless it's a variation of the classic AABA form (verse with the title in the first or last line, followed by another of the same followed by a section with a different melody, then back to the melody of the first verse) like Billy Joel's "Just the Way You Are." Another exception might be an AAA form entered in a folk (but not country) category. An AAA form is a story-telling form that uses the same melody in every section, a form not well suited to mass market radio formats because it tends to get too monotonous.

2. The title doesn't appear in the chorus or first or last line of the verse. This commercial consideration is important in the marketing of a song because if potential buyers can't identify a song they have heard, sales may be lost.

3. Cliché lyrics. A judge may hear over one hundred songs at a judging session and will certainly hear the same cliché phrases over and over again. If you've heard it before, don't use it.

4. Little or no melodic change between verses, chorus and bridge. You must hold a judge's attention, and the melodic contrast is one of the best techniques to help you do it. If you can't hold the judge's attention, you won't hold an audience's either.

IS THE CONTEST LEGIT?

A history of take-the-money-and-run contests make it important to be on the lookout for some distinguishing factors that help you recognize the legitimate ones. Here are some things to look for:

1. If a contest has been in operation for more than a year, they should be willing to provide you with a list of previous winners.

2. If they offer you merchandise prizes, they should be able to prove to you that they have either purchased them or, with an affidavit from the manufacturer, that the merchandise has been donated. Note: Most manufacturers no longer directly donate equipment, but may work in conjunction with a local music store to make it available to the contest in consideration of publicity.

3. If the contest offers a cash prize, they should be able to offer proof that the money is in an escrow account that may only be distributed to winners. A common downfall of contests is to promise prize money with the honest hope that money received from entries will exceed the prize amount by enough to cover all expenses and profit. This is a very risky gamble because it is expensive

to get enough publicity to ensure that many entries, and once a contest fails to provide prizes on time, its reputation has been destroyed.

4. The individuals responsible for the contest should be listed in the advertising, and there should be an address (street number) and phone number where they can be reached.

5. The contest officers, owners, representatives, judges and their families should be ineligible to enter the contest.

6. Prize schedules and amounts as well as entry deadlines, deadlines for notification of winners and awarding of prizes should be clearly listed on the application. If a deadline becomes impossible to meet, a predetermined process for notifying contestants should be implemented. New deadlines must be clearly stated.

7. Judges of the contest must be music industry professionals with proven experience in judging and critiquing songs and, hopefully, in a position to further your career.

8. Don't enter contests in which your entry becomes the property of the contest. In fact, look for a phrase that specifically says that it doesn't. However, the contest should have the right to play the song, print it or use your name and photo for promotional purposes. Your career benefits directly from that publicity and is one of the unstated prizes for a winner.

There is another caution related to ownership of your entry or winning song. Every year there are at least two or three individuals who want to get into the music publishing business and think that a great new way to find songs and finance their businesses is to have a contest and offer the winner a publishing contract. Sometimes they'll form a record company and their first recording artist will sing your song. Savvy writers don't enter these contests for several reasons:

1. If you believe in the commercial potential of your songs, the worst prize you can imagine is that your song will be owned by an inexperienced and unconnected new publisher whose only means of financing a company and finding songs is to hold a contest.

2. Legitimate publishers never charge you to screen your songs. It is part of the business of a music publisher to find material and convince the writer that he can represent your song better than anyone else. So to set themselves up as someone you would "automatically" want to publish your songs, without a track record or connections, is arrogant, to say the least. Frankly, under certain circumstances, there may be writers who should not even sign with well-established major publishers because, in their individual circumstances, it may not be in their best interest.

FINDING CONTESTS

Contests come and go, so a listing here may be out of date by the time you read it. The guidelines listed above should help to keep you out of trouble. There are, however, some well-established sources through which you can find out about contests. A great source for international competitions is FIDOF, the international federation of festival organizations. FIDOF is a nonprofit organization with contacts to over 1,600 festivals and cultural events in seventy-two countries around the world and releases a monthly bulletin for members about those events. The competitions are for performers and songwriters. You can reach them at (818) 789-7536.

Songwriter's Market has a section, "Contests and Awards," that lists most of the well-established regularly held contests. You'll also find information on the requirements and purposes of the contests.

Your local songwriters organization is another good place to find out about songwriting competitions since they're sure to be on the mailing list of anyone promoting the contest.

In addition to songwriting competitions, there are always many contests for individual performers and bands. One of the most visible is Soundcheck, the Yamaha rock music competition that you can find out about through your local music store. In fact, music stores are the best places to find out about band competitions both locally and nationally.

PRIZES

You will partially base your decision to enter a competition on the lure of the money or hardware offered to winners. Customarily, a grand prize is awarded to an overall winner and first, second, third and more prizes are awarded in each stylistic category. In addition, honorable mention certificates may be awarded to songs that judges felt deserved special consideration but didn't make the finals.

SAMPLE ENTRY FORM FOR BILLBOARD SONG CONTEST

OFFICIAL RULES AND PRIZES

1. Send the following with each entry:
   a. Completed entry form (or photocopy). All signatures must be original.
   b. One audio cassette recording for the song contest or VHS video cassette recording for the video category including your name and address on cassette. Only VHS video cassettes accepted for the video category.
   c. Lyrics typed or printed legibly in English. In Latin category, lyrics may be in Spanish with an English translation. In Jazz category, lyrics not required.
   d. Check or money order made payable to 5th Annual Billboard Song Contest, or credit card approval for $15.00 (U.S.) for each song or video submitted.
   Contestant's name, address and song title must appear on each item along with any co-authors names (if applicable).
2. Mail entries to: 5th Annual Billboard Song Contest, P.O. Box 35346, Tulsa, OK 74153-0346. **ENTRIES MUST BE RECEIVED NO LATER THAN AUG. 31, 1993.**
3. **Songwriting Entries:** Each song submitted must be contestant's original work. Songs may be no longer than five minutes.
   Video production entries: Songs do not have to be original work. Video may be no longer than ten minutes. Video production prizes will be awarded to the video producers/directors named on the winning entry forms.
   Contestant may enter as many songs as he/she wishes, but each song must have its own entry form and be recorded on separate cassette accompanied by typed or printed lyric sheet. Check or money order must reflect the total number of entries submitted. Contestant may enter in more than one category; each submission constitutes a separate entry, requiring its own entry form, entry fee, cassette and lyrics. Entry fee is not refundable. Copyright registration not required. If song is registered, contestants must put copyright notices on entries and file under U.S. copyright laws. Billboard Song Contest not responsible for entries late, lost, damaged, misdirected, mailed with insufficient postage, stolen or misappropriated. **CASSETTES AND LYRICS WILL NOT BE RETURNED.**
4. **SONGWRITING PRIZES** and estimated maximum retail value: **One (1) Grand Prize** – $5,000 cash, Gibson Chet Atkins SST Guitar, approx. $1,199 value, Dean Markley K150 amplifier approx. $500 value, BMG Publishing contract for winning song.
   Six (6) First Prizes (one in each category excluding the Grand Prize winner) $1,000 cash, Gibson Chet Atkins SST Guitar, approx. $1,199 value, BMG Publishing contract for winning song.
   Seven (7) Second Prizes (one in each category) Gibson Epiphone PR-350 Guitar, approx. $363 value.
   The top 500 songwriters in the contest will receive a pair of BluBlocker Sunglasses, approx. $60 value.
   2,500 Honorable Mention Certificates of Achievement to writers judged among best signed by Billboard Publisher.
   VIDEO PRODUCTION PRIZES and estimated maximum retail value:

ates, Dean Markley Strings, Inc., Laughton Promotional Marketing and their families, subsidiaries, affiliates, advertising, public relations and promotion agencies are not eligible.
6. Winners will be selected by a Blue Ribbon Panel under supervision of Laughton Promotional Marketing, an independent judging agency whose decision in all matters pertaining to contest is final. Blue Ribbon Panel will be comprised of noted professional songwriters and other music industry professionals who may be substituted due to availability or at Contest discretion. Semi-finalists will be selected for consideration by Blue Ribbon Panel by preliminary panels supervised by songwriting professionals. All song entries judged equally on Originality, Lyrics, Melody and Composition. Production and performance quality not considered. No duplicate winners in a single category. Video production prize winners entries judged equally on: Creativity, Originality, Concept, Visual Technique and Aesthetic Composition. Winners will be determined by 1/31/94. No transfer and no substitution of prizes except as necessary due to availability, in which case prize of equal or greater value will be awarded. Division of prizes among co-authors is responsibility of winners and awarded to first name on entry form. All prizes will be awarded. Taxes responsibility of winners. Void where prohibited. All federal, state and local laws and regulations apply.
7. Winners will be notified by mail and must sign and return affidavit of eligibility/liability/publicity release within 14 days of notification date. Song contest affidavit includes statement that winner's song is original work and he/she holds all rights to song. Failure to sign and return such affidavit within 14 days or provision of false/inaccurate information therein will result in immediate disqualification and alternate winner will be selected. Affidavits of winners under 18 years of age at time of award must be countersigned by parent or legal guardian. Affidavits subject to verification by Laughton Promotional Marketing and its agents. By accepting prize the winner releases sponsors from all liability regarding prizes awarded. Entry constitutes permission to use winners' names, likenesses and voices for future advertising and publicity purposes without additional compensation.
   FOR ADDITIONAL ENTRY FORMS, OR WINNERS LIST, SEND SELF-ADDRESSED STAMPED ENVELOPE TO: 5TH ANNUAL BILLBOARD SONG CONTEST (SPECIFY ENTRY FORMS OR WINNERS LISTS) P.O. BOX 35346, TULSA, OK 74153-0346. REQUESTS FOR ENTRY FORMS MUST BE RECEIVED BY JULY 31, 1993. REQUESTS FOR WINNERS LIST MUST BE RECEIVED BY JANUARY 15, 1994. IF YOU HAVE ANY QUESTIONS REGARDING CONTEST CALL 918-627-0351, MON-FRI BETWEEN 9AM AND 5PM CENTRAL TIME.

I certify that I have read and understand the 5th Annual Billboard Song Contest Official Rules and I accept the terms and conditions of participation ... official rules. (If entrant is under ... t or guardian is required).

_____
Date

_____
Date

Choose your category wisely—if you're unsure, enter the same song in two categories

BILLBOARD MAGAZINE IS SEARCHING FOR NEW CREATIVE TALENT!

Enter the Fifth Annual Billboard Song Contest for the opportunity to win cash, music contracts and more!

SONG AND VIDEO ENTRIES NOW ACCEPTED
Video directors can enter for video production prizes

Enter The Billboard SONG CONTEST

For each entry you submit a completed entry form, lyrics typed or printed legibly in English, an audio cassette for the song contest or VHS video cassette for the video category and a check, money order, VISA or MasterCard payment authorization for the $15 per entry fee. Make sure your name, address and song title appear on each item submitted. See official rules on reverse side for details.

NAME _____

ADDRESS _____

CITY _____ STATE _____ ZIP _____

PHONE NUMBER ( ) _____ AGE _____

WHERE DID YOU OBTAIN ENTRY FORM _____

CHECK ONE: MC ☐ VISA ☐ CARD NUMBER _____

EXP. DATE _____ SIGNATURE _____
(if paying by credit card)

Check or money order for $15 per entry should be made payable to: **5th Annual Billboard Song Contest**

SONG CATEGORIES: ☐ ROCK ☐ COUNTRY ☐ LATIN ☐ R&B or RAP
☐ POP ☐ JAZZ ☐ GOSPEL/CONTEMPORARY CHRISTIAN

Song Title: _____

For video production prize eligibility, enter name and address of video producer/director here: _____

We will add your name to our mailing list for Song Contest information and music/entertainment industry opportunities. If you **do not** want to receive this material check here: ☐

MAIL YOUR ENTRY TO: **5TH ANNUAL BILLBOARD SONG CONTEST**
P.O. BOX 35346, TULSA, OK 74153-0346

Be sure to sign the back of this form after carefully reading the official rules. **This entry form may be photocopied as needed.**

We thank our co-sponsors **BMG Music, Gibson Guitars, Dean Markley Strings** and **BluBlocker Sunglasses** for their participation in this contest.

1   2   3   4   5   6   8   9   10   11   12   13

CHAPTER 12

KEEPING RECORDS

N ow that you have read through this book and are ready to put into practice everything you have learned, there is still one skill left to master. It is not unique to songwriting or the music industry. Successful people in every field usually have mastered it. In our business, behind creativity and perseverance it is probably the most important element to you attaining your goal. What is it? (Don't let the word scare you.) Organization.

For many musicians, this is a frightening concept. It may be because you feel that it stifles the creative process or that you were born messy. Whatever your excuse is, it is no more than that—an excuse! If you intend to seriously pursue your career, you must organize your approach. What you will find in this section are some very simple and practical solutions for getting organized.

THE IMPORTANCE OF ORGANIZATION

As you learned in the previous chapters, there is a considerable number of companies and individuals to whom you can submit your material. It does not take long for the novice to learn that submitting one song to one place one at a time, and then waiting for a reply is a waste of your valuable time. Most, if not all, veterans in the business have a number of projects on the go at any given moment. For some writers it would not be unusual to pitch a song to twenty or so "clients" and do that with ten or fifteen songs a year. But whether they are pitching one song or one hundred, most writers share a common bad habit; they do not keep any formal record of their attempts to place their material.

You can ask almost any writer the details about the process of writing one of their songs, months or even years after the fact, and they will be able to recount to you what the inspiration was for the song, where they were when they wrote it and what they thought to be its chances of success. But ask that same writer when they mailed off their latest tape or even to list all the people to whom they sent it and you will be greeted by a blank stare. How many times have you heard a version of this conversation?

"Are you having any luck with that new song of yours?"

"I haven't heard back from anyone yet!"

"When did you send it off?"

"Oh, it was last week sometime . . . No! It was almost two weeks. I think."

Another common problem is that if you do receive a reply that has some comments pro or con or just some friendly advice, you tend to carry the letter around for a few days and then file it. Unfortunately for most songwriters, "filing it" means shoving it in the back of some drawer never to be seen again until you move.

What you are losing track of is not just a song, a comment or a name, but an opportunity. Even rejection presents you with the chance to advance your career because you are learning! This method is not just a bookkeeping exercise, it is an educational system. If you follow through on your record keeping you are going to learn a lot about your songs and the people you send them to. This knowledge will allow you to make better use of your time as a writer. Let's see how an organizational method can help.

THE BASIC MATERIALS

Before we actually discuss one particular method of storing your materials, it should be pointed out that in this, too, you can be creative. We have chosen to tell you about the ring binder method because the materials needed are generally available to everyone and the space required is minimal. That is not to say, however, that this is the only method of storing records. You may wish to use an accordion file commonly found in business stores. They can be used alphabetically or you may set up your own filing system based on months, companies, cities or whatever you wish. This also holds true for using large filing cabinets if you have the space.

Another excellent method is the computer. Just as the sample forms at the end of this chapter were created on a computer, you can create your own forms and your own database. There are many excellent database programs that allow you to create your own parameters. If you have a scanner, all you need to do is scan the forms provided in this book and you're off to the races. (A note of caution: Back up all your work. If you put all your forms and information to hard disk and it fails, you are in big trouble without a back-up copy.)

As an example, we will describe the binder method. What you will end up with is a three ring binder with several divider cards in it. The divider cards are going to separate the various categories you have chosen to include in

your system. Here is a suggested list of categories. Do not hesitate to create
your own!
   • Industry Information Sheets
   • Song History
   • Call Sheets
   • Copyright Registrations
   • Demo Files

If you do choose to use this method, you can copy the sample forms and
use them in your notebook as they are, or you can design your own. Whichever
way you do it, you'll be making progress. The more blanks you fill in on your
sheets, the closer you are to your goal. Attitude is the name of the game.

The first thing you will need is a regular-sized three-ring binder. Try to
buy the kind with the square rather than the round rings. You will find as you
fill up your binder that the square rings make it easier to turn the pages and
you will not have the problem of tearing some sheets out by accident. Also,
you might spend some extra money and buy a binder with a substantial cover
to it. It will protect your records much better than a paper or light plastic cover
would. Next, buy some file separators for the various categories of records that
you will keep. You will find it helpful, once you have marked your separators
with the appropriate categories, to go to a printer or even to a local Mailbox
franchise and have them laminated. This adds more weight to them, making
it easier to turn and find your place, and it also helps to preserve the sheets
in-between the different categories. Start out with just the minimum number
of categories. It would be a shame to make a mess of the book by trying to
keep track of too much at once.

Take your category sheets and place them in your notebook. You will have
to decide how many you'll need, but don't overdo it. Ten sheets per category
is reasonable. It is also a good idea to use a heavier than usual weight of
paper. You want something that can stand up to constant handling.

You will need some way of circulating the active and inactive files. For
this purpose, you may want to have a fixed file cabinet or accordion file that
is dedicated to your music business. Putting your sheets loose in a drawer or
in with other business defeats the whole purpose of this system.

After some time, you may have enough information to rearrange your
binder. Every six months is a reasonable time to evaluate how your system is
working.

Now let's look at some categories and how they can be used.

THE INDUSTRY INFORMATION SHEET

It's a "Who You Know" business. The first place to store your information
has as much to do with people as with songs (see sample, page 141). This is

because it is the people you know who give you the opportunity. You must keep track of them and of their responses to your material on a sheet similar to the industry information sheet. You have heard many stories about how someone got a break because of someone they knew. This is your way to get to know someone. Record each call or meeting that produces an acceptance, rejection or even a "send me some more." Try to collect as many names as possible and keep them up to date.

This is how you start to build your important network of contacts. Because each submission reply will be at your fingertips, you can ask questions based on these replies. For example, if you receive a comment from one person to whom you have submitted several songs that indicates that they like one of your songs except for the bridge, you might ask them to recommend a current song as an example of a good bridge. You then file this in that person's information sheet under "Comments," and the next time you contact them you let them know you followed their advice and have incorporated it into your new song.

When you receive a phone call from someone to whom you have sent your tape, it is usually an indication of strong interest in either you, a song or both. This is another great time to have your files up to date so that you can turn to the person's name and refresh your memory as to who they are, what you sent them and when you sent it. Having this information at your fingertips helps you organize your thoughts and then your questions and comments to them.

Let's assume you have been sending out tapes and receiving replies for six months. This will give you a database of at least ten to fifteen names with a couple of replies from each person. Review the responses to see who has given you the best response (these could be either positive comments or detailed criticisms), remove any names that have not been productive, then add an equal number of new names to your files. Do this every six months or so to get the best results. This way your mailing list won't get out of hand and you will be sending the material where it is doing the most good.

After a few submissions to a certain person, you can study their responses at a glance and decide how valuable or suitable they are for you. If you find that they are consistently complimenting your work, perhaps it is time to give them a call and try to get some first-hand direction. If you see that they have consistently rejected your work with a "no comment" or have indicated a preference for a certain type of material that you are neither interested in or adept at, it is time to take that person off your list and concentrate on those who have given you a positive response.

One last point about the Information Sheet. It can also be used to record personal information on the individual. Career moves, hobbies, favorite acts —

all of this is valuable information. It helps you to get to know them and it will provide several conversation starters.

For example, let's say that you send off a tape to a publisher who sent back a note asking you to give him a call. You called but your conversation was interrupted because he had to leave the office early and take his son to a ball game. He said to call back early next week. When you call the next Monday, the conversation could go two ways.

Songwriter: Hello, is Mike Publisher in?

Publisher: Speaking.

Songwriter: Yes, Mike, this is Sam Writer calling. I called about my song "Believe in Me."

Publisher: "Believe in Me"? Refresh my memory, Sam.

Songwriter: You sent me a note saying you liked the chorus.

You see, you are already off to a bad start. You have to reintroduce yourself and try to re-establish the connection you thought you had previously made. Now try this for an alternative.

Songwriter: Hello, is Mike Publisher in?

Publisher: Speaking.

Songwriter: Yes, Mike, it's Sam Writer calling. We started to have a discussion about my song "Believe in Me," but you had to rush off and take your son to a ball game. You asked me to . . .

Publisher: Yes, Sam, I remember.

Songwriter: Did he win?

Publisher: Worst team in the league, Sam, but they have a lot of fun.

In this conversation, you have accomplished two things. You have refreshed his memory and you are now starting to establish a stronger connection than in the first conversation, when you simply tried to resume your business discussion. Remember, these people have normal lives outside of music, too, and it is in your interest to be able to converse with them about other interests.

PROSPECTS SHEET

You may want to think about starting your "Who You Know" file with local people (see sample, page 142). Not everyone lives in a music center or even close to one. I know it's very tempting to open an industry sourcebook and start writing to the biggest names you can identify. That may be exciting, and you may be one of the lucky ones to hit paydirt immediately, but more likely, you will have to pay your dues like everyone else. Part of that payment might as well be made right in your own area. It will give you some good practice at approaching people and it will probably generate at least several meaningful contracts.

You can find your first "Who You Knows" at your local music stores or through recording studios. Don't just walk in and start pumping them for information. Spend a few dollars. Buy some equipment and ask some questions. Rent some demo time and find out who else is using the studio. Contact the local radio stations and major retail outlets and find out the name of any record company people that they know. The main thing is, it's a beginning. You would be surprised to find out how many major players in the music business made some of their most important contacts at the start of their careers, often in their old hometowns!

To help you out, you may want to include a "Prospects Section" in your notebook. Here you can list artists, record companies, publishers, producers and managers who may prove to be important contacts. As you submit your materials to them and receive their replies, you can move their names from the Prospects Sheet to the Information Sheet.

SONG HISTORY SHEET

It is a good idea to keep track of where each song stands on the submissions track (see sample, page 143). It may seem redundant at first to have two entries for one reply but you will soon understand the advantage of the song history section. Whereas the information and prospect sections will help you keep track of and learn about people in the industry, the song history section will provide you with a snapshot of that song and your efforts on its behalf.

The date at the top should be the first date you actually mail a song out. If you start to fill up your files with songs that you have not yet mailed out, they will simply clutter up your active song file.

After the title, include the style category. This is helpful because some songs can be pitched in more than one category. You may have a different sheet for each incarnation of the song. This will be determined by your song-casting (the art of matching an artist with a song). If your selection of artists is Tanya Tucker, Michelle Wright and Cassandra Vasik, your style of song obviously must be country. You may have a different demo of the song in a rock style that could be pitched to Allanah Miles, Bonnie Raitt and Kim Carnes.

The shares section in the sample Song History Sheet is there to remind you what the writing arrangements were for that particular song. Just underneath those is a check off for whether you have copies of lyrics, tapes, etc. ready for distribution.

Finally, with this section, you will have a place to record the names of those to whom you have pitched your song. At a glance, you will be able to see your progress (or lack thereof) in sending your materials out. "Who did I send that song to?" or "When did I send it?" have both been answered. Most importantly, you will be able to redirect or rework your songs based on the information you compile in just a few months. Your summary of the general reaction to this song can be written at the bottom of the page. Eventually these written comments will help you pinpoint the strengths and weaknesses of your material.

BUSINESS CARDS

Most veterans of the music industry have had the pleasure of discovering old business cards in suit jackets, wallets and tape boxes years after having met someone. It is the rare bird in this business who actually has one of those nice, slim business card holders and keeps it up to date. That's a pity because we all seem to waste a lot of time searching for phone numbers and addresses that were literally handed to us. I have a cheap and easy solution for you! Go to any major stationery or office supply outlet and you will find 8½″ × 11″ clear plastic sheets made to hold business cards. The sheets usually have three holes to fit into a three-ring notebook. Once again, the reason for this is to have everything organized and in one place. You can organize the sheets into different categories depending on your preference. This can be done by location (local, national, international), type of business (record company, publisher, producer) or individuals (producers, artist managers).

COPYRIGHT

If you are determined to be organized, you may find all sorts of categories that need looking after. Most of us understand the value of copyright protection, but, once again, we don't seem to keep track of whether we've registered the song, when we registered it and where the registration forms are. Your notebook should contain this information (see sample, page 144). If you wish to keep the actual documents registering your copyrights in your industry file, then while you are at the stationery store, pick up a plastic sleeve in which to insert each registration. In any case, a simple copyright sheet such as the one I have used as an example will be helpful.

THE DEMO FILE SHEET

One of the great tortures of songwriting is making the demo. Another torture is keeping track of it. How many times have you said "I know it's around here someplace!" Let's suppose you want to find a song that you started working on last week. Your first chore is to find the tape! Next you begin to search on the tape for the right take. By using your notebook filing system, you are able to zero in on your song in a much faster and less aggravating way (see sample, page 145). (Have you ever decided *not* to do some work on a song just because you dread the thought of trying to find your last version?)

Here's a good suggestion for both your works in progress and copies of your finished demo. Instead of buying full-length cassettes and putting your tune who knows where on one of the thousand tapes lying around the room, take time to search out a tape supplier who will provide you with custom-length cassettes. Buy a box of c-10s, a bunch of labels and pop a new tape into your machine each time you record a demo. Whip a label on it and file. One tape, one song. It saves a lot of aggravation. Do not try to file by tape number or location; that will eventually lead to a system in disarray! Label all your tapes the moment you have finished recording them. Unmarked cassettes are like rabbits; they multiply at amazing speeds. The hours we have all spent listening to the same tapes over and over again! If you don't know how to label it, it's not worth keeping.

Each individual song should have a sheet of its own, similar to the sample. These sheets should be alphabetically filed in your notebook and will help you keep track of where you have filed each tape. If you must use a regular length tape, this sheet will also help you find the take you are looking for on the tape.

THE BEGINNING

No matter how long you are a songwriter, you will always feel thrilled when someone accepts your song. The words "Let's do a deal" or "I got a cover on your tune" are the real music in a songwriter's life. Those opportunities are most often the result of long and careful cultivation by professionals who understand that writing is half the work. Making contacts is what brings it all home. Get going!

SAMPLE INDUSTRY INFORMATION SHEET

Name _____
       (First)   (Middle)   (Last)

Company _____

Address _____
       (Number)   (Street)

       _____
       (City)   (State/Prov)

                          _____
                          (Country)   (Zip)

Phone:

Area Code _____

Work _____ Home _____ Car _____ Fax _____

Reminders _____

         _____

         _____

1. Date   Song/Project   Result

_____   _____   _____

Comment: _____

2. Date   Song/Project   Result

_____   _____   _____

Comment: _____

3. Date   Song/Project   Result

_____   _____   _____

Comment: _____

4. Date   Song/Project   Result

_____   _____   _____

Comment: _____

SAMPLE PROSPECTS SHEET

City: _____

Prospects

Artist   Record Company

1. _____   1. _____

2. _____   2. _____

3. _____   3. _____

4. _____   4. _____

5. _____   5. _____

6. _____   6. _____

7. _____   7. _____

8. _____   8. _____

Publisher   Producer   Manager

1. _____   1. _____   1. _____

2. _____   2. _____   2. _____

3. _____   3. _____   3. _____

4. _____   4. _____   4. _____

5. _____   5. _____   5. _____

6. _____   6. _____   6. _____

7. _____   7. _____   7. _____

8. _____   8. _____   8. _____

SAMPLE SONG HISTORY SHEET

Song History

_____
(date)

Title _____

Style _____

Song Casting 1. _____ 2. _____ 3. _____

Writer(s)	Share(s)	Publisher(s)	Share(s)
_____	_____	_____	____
_____	_____	_____	____
_____	_____	_____	____
_____	_____	_____	____

Lyrics ___ Lead Sheet ___ Demo ___ Record ___

Pitched to:　1. _____
　　　　　　　　　　(see information sheet)

　　　　　　　2. _____
　　　　　　　　　　(see information sheet)

　　　　　　　3. _____
　　　　　　　　　　(see information sheet)

　　　　　　　4. _____
　　　　　　　　　　(see information sheet)

　　　　　　　5. _____
　　　　　　　　　　(see information sheet)

　　　　　　　6. _____
　　　　　　　　　　(see information sheet)

Notes and Comments

SAMPLE COPYRIGHT REGISTRATIONS SHEET

Copyright Registration

Song	Submitted — Date — Received		Owner
_____	_____	_____	_____
_____	_____	_____	_____
_____	_____	_____	_____
_____	_____	_____	_____
_____	_____	_____	_____
_____	_____	_____	_____
_____	_____	_____	_____
_____	_____	_____	_____
_____	_____	_____	_____
_____	_____	_____	_____
_____	_____	_____	_____
_____	_____	_____	_____
_____	_____	_____	_____
_____	_____	_____	_____
_____	_____	_____	_____
_____	_____	_____	_____
_____	_____	_____	_____
_____	_____	_____	_____
_____	_____	_____	_____

SAMPLE DEMO FILE SHEET

Demo File

Song: _____

Cassette _____ DAT _____

2-track _____ 4-track _____ 8-track _____ 16-track _____ 24-track _____

Tape Storage Location _____

File Number: _____

Tape Contents:	Code or Counter Location
1. _____	_____
2. _____	_____
3. _____	_____
4. _____	_____
5. _____	_____
6. _____	_____
7. _____	_____
8. _____	_____
9. _____	_____
10. _____	_____
11. _____	_____
12. _____	_____
13. _____	_____
14. _____	_____
15. _____	_____

Notes

CONTRIBUTORS

ANNE M. BOWLING is a freelance writer and editor. She's has contributed to several Writer's Digest books and was the assistant editor for *Songwriter's Market*. Ann interviewed Rosalie Calabrese of the American Composer's Alliance, among others, for her chapter in this book. She is the author of chapter ten.

JOHN BRAHENY is the co-founder/director (with Len Chandler) of the Los Angeles Songwriters Showcase, a national nonprofit service organization founded in 1971. He's been a musician, performer, songwriter, recording artist, film composer, commercial jingle producer, educator, author and journalist. He is the author of *The Craft and Business of Songwriting* (Writer's Digest Books). He has taught "Songwriting Business," "Song Evaluation" and "Music Publishing" at Grove School of Music in Los Angeles and is publisher/editor of the *Songwriters Musepaper*, a monthly magazine. He is the author of chapter eleven.

ROBERT COLSON is an investigative reporter, songwriter, musician, actor and screenwriter. He's a regular contributing writer and air personality for *Super Driver* and has been published in *Music Row* magazine and *Nashville Business & Lifestyles*. As an actor, he's appeared in several movies, including *Sweet Dreams*, *Ernest Goes to Jail* and *Last Days of Frank and Jesse James*, and has been a cast member of the Amerikahaus. He played bass and sang backup vocals for "Mama" Cass Elliot, performed concerts with Bob Dylan, Joan Baez, Carly Simon, the Smothers Brothers, Peter, Paul and Mary, and toured with Grand Ole Opry stars Buck Trent, Johnny Russell, Jan Howard and Justin Tubb. He's produced benefit concerts featuring Emmylou Harris, Geraldo Rivera, David Keith and others. He is the co-author of chapter five.

LIBBE S. HALEVY is an award-winning playwright, librettist and lyricist with over fifty productions to her credit. Her musicals include *Kazoo* and *Aar-*

mageddon: A Virtual Reality; her plays include *Shattered Secrets*, *Sexual Sushi*, *Thanksgiving* and *Marilyn: The Final Session*. She is co-director of Broadway on Sunset, a musical theater development organization headquartered in Los Angeles, where she teaches courses in libretto and collaboration, facilitates readings and workshops, and consults on musical works-in-progress. Halevy is a member of the Dramatists Guild, the Alliance of Los Angeles Playwrights, Women in Theater and Theater LA. She is the co-author of chapter nine.

KEVIN KAUFMAN is the founder and co-director of Broadway on Sunset, the West Coast's only musical theater writer's organization offering programs in craft, business and development. Broadway on Sunset is sponsored by the Songwriters Guild of America with Tony Award-winning director/choreographer Grover Dale serving as creative advisor. Kaufman, a musical dramatist and theater producer, has composed four original musicals, two published by Hartmut Lang-Edition, Berlin, Germany. He studied arranging and composition at the Grove School of Music in Los Angeles and received his B.A. in music from the City College of New York. He is a member of the Dramatists Guild, ASCAP and the Songwriters Guild of America. He is the co-author of chapter nine.

DAN KIMPEL has been a songwriter, performer, producer, promoter, publicist and manager in his long career in the music business. He currently operates an artist management firm in Los Angeles and is advertising director for the Los Angeles Songwriters Showcase, an organization dedicated to serving and educating songwriters. Dan is the author of the book *Networking in the Music Business* (Writer's Digest Books). He is the author of chapters one and four.

PAT LUBOFF is co-author with her husband, Pete, of *88 Songwriting Wrongs & How to Right Them* (Writer's Digest Books) and is co-editor of *L.A. Record* for the Los Angeles chapter of the National Academy of Recording Arts and Sciences, Inc. (the Grammy organization) and the California Copyright Conference newsletter. Pat and Pete live in Los Angeles and have traveled throughout the West to teach songwriting workshops. Their songs have been recorded by Patti LaBelle (gold album) and Bobby Womack (No. 2 on *Billboard*'s Black Music chart), and have been featured in the John Travolta movie, *Experts*. She is the author of chapters two, six and seven.

ARGIE MANOLIS is a senior at Kent State University, majoring in English and magazine journalism. She helped edit this book and wrote chapter three as an intern with Writer's Digest Books.

ANDREW MARK is founder and president of Philadelphia Music Works, Inc., a producer of musical image packages, or "jingles," for radio advertisers. Since the company's founding in 1972, it has produced more than six thousand customer jingles for more than six hundred radio stations worldwide. Mark is also president of Canary Productions and president/CEO of TriCities Broadcasting. Andrew, his wife Cynthia and his two children live in Villanova, Pennsylvania. He is the author of chapter eight.

MARJIE MCGRAW, a Nashville-based entertainment journalist, is Nashville's correspondent for *Weekly Variety*; edits "Nashville Hotline" for ZAPNEWS, a radio newsfeed to major market radio stations; edits *Super Driver*, Comdata's three-hour monthly audio magazine; is an editorial consultant for the Toronto-based live radio show, "Today's Country"; wrote the country music news for NBC's *John & Leeza From Hollywood*; and currently writes the country music news for the syndicated *Joan Rivers Show*. Her work has been published in *Ladies Home Journal*, *Saturday Evening Post*, *First*, *Country America*, *Country Music*, *Complete Woman* and over a dozen other publications. Her celebrity interviews are syndicated on Olympia Broadcasting's "Country Calendar" and Ricky Skagg's "Simple Life." She is co-author of chapter five.

TERRY MCMANUS is currently the chairman of the board of the Songwriters Association of Canada and a professor of music business and contracts in the Music Industry Arts program at Fanshawe College in London, Ontario. He is also the author of the Songhound system of keeping records. Terry has been a recording artist for A&M Records and Capitol Records. As a songwriter, he has placed material with Irving/Almo Music, Warner Music and Rondor Music in England. Currently, he continues to write children's music for television as well as working on various other music projects. He is the author of chapter twelve.

GLOSSARY

AAA form: a song form in which every verse has the same melody; often used for songs that tell a story.

AABA form: also called the verse/bridge structure. A classic song form with three verses, all of the same melody, which each begin or end with the title of the song. The bridge, sandwiched between the last two verses, is a different melody.

advance: money paid to a songwriter, recording artist, etc., before regular royalty payment begins. Advances are deducted from royalties.

advertising medium: in advertising, the device that "carries" the message to the listener or viewer; e.g., radio, television, etc.

A&R Department: stands for Artist and Repertoire Department, the record company department that finds and develops new artists and matches songs with artists.

ASCAP: stands for American Society of Composers, Authors and Publishers. The oldest performing rights organization, founded in 1914. Will accept any published writer as a member. Also accepts associate members who have not yet been published. Minimal annual membership fee.

bin loop master tape: a ½" recording tape that is copied directly from the master tape and used in mass duplication of tapes; has "tones" at the beginning and end of a series of songs, which tell the duplication machines when to start and stop recording.

black box: theater without fixed stage or seating arrangements, capable of a variety of formations. Usually a small space, often attached to a major theater complex, used for workshops or experimental works calling for small casts and limited sets.

BMI: stands for Broadcast Music, Inc., the largest performing arts organization. Will accept any published writer as a member. No annual membership fee; minimal one-time fee to join.

book: see *libretto.*

bridge: a section of a song that is neither a verse nor a chorus but connects verses, choruses or verses and choruses. It is musically and lyrically different from the rest of the song.

broadcast account: an advertising account with a company that advertises over the radio, network television or cable television.

business manager: professional hired to handle the financial aspects of an artist's career.

canned music: music that has been written and produced with no specific purpose in mind. The music is usually placed on a CD collection in music libraries, where it can be purchased by radio and TV commercial, film, video and audio producers.

cassette shell: portion of a cassette that holds the tape.

chorus: (1) The section of a song that repeats both musically and lyrically. It usually begins or ends with the title of the song and encompasses the song's theme. (2) In a play or musical, the characters that are not central to the plot but help set the scene and enhance the story line and the musical arrangements.

chrome tape: type of audiotape that records and plays back with more high frequencies than normal bias tape. Of the common types of cassette tapes, it is considered second to metal tape in quality of duplication.

collaboration: two or more artists, writers, etc., working together on a single project; for instance, a playwright and a songwriter creating a musical together.

controlled venue showcase: a private performance geared to presenting an act to a potential buyer.

copyright: exclusive legal right giving the creator of a song, musical, composition, etc. the power to control the publishing reproduction and selling of the work.

DAT: stands for Digital Audio Tape. A tape that can record and play back digitally encoded sound, is smaller and produces a better sound than conventional cassettes, and is often used as a master when cassette tapes are mass duplicated.

demo tape: a demonstration tape submitted to a producer, manager, director, etc., to give them a taste of one's talent.

Dolby C: A system used to limit tape noise and increase dynamic range in analog magnetic recording.

engineer: specially trained professional who operates all recording requipment.

experimental musical: musical that includes a form, theme or musical style not usually seen in theatrical performances.

fly space: area above a stage from which set pieces are lowered and raised during a performance.

high bias tape: see *chrome tape.*

high position tape: see *chrome tape.*

indies: small, independent recording companies, publishers and producers.

J-card: cassette box insert that lists length of songs, pertinent publishing and performing rights information, etc.

jingle: a short song used to enhance advertisements on television or radio.

label: (1) A recording company. (2) The brand name of the records a particular recording company produces.

lead sheet: a written version of a song, including the melody, the chord symbols and the lyrics.

libretto: the "book" or script of a musical that tells the story; sets structure, defines characters and indicates where musical numbers can be placed. It does not include the actual lyrics and musical arrangements of the songs.

lithographer: a professional who screens photographs.

live showcases: performances geared toward presenting an act to potential buyers, either in a public or a private show.

logo: a specially designed representation of an artist or band. Also called a *stamp.*

metal tape: tape made of chromium dioxide particles. The most expensive of the three common types of cassette tape. Metal tape is considered to have the highest level of duplication and is able to record and play back at higher decibel levels than chrome or normal bias tapes.

MIDI studio: stands for musical instrument digital interface studio. A studio using a universal interface that allows musical instruments to communicate with each other through computers.

music library: a business that purchases canned music, which can then be bought by producers of radio and TV commercials, films,

videos and audiovisual productions.

music publisher: company that evaluates songs for commercial potential, finds artists to record them, and finds other uses for them (such as TV or film). The company collects income generated by the songs and protects copyrights.

needledrop: refers to a type of music library. A needledrop music library is a licensed library that allows producers to "borrow" music on a rate schedule. The price depends on how the music will be used.

normal bias tape: of the three common types of cassette tape, it has the lowest range of cassette duplication. Most prerecorded tapes are normal bias.

O-card: four-sided sleeves that are shrink-wrapped to completely surround cassette tapes. Often used in place of cassette boxes on cassette singles.

pay to play: refers to a type of show in which a promoter books three or more bands in a night and sells the bands advance tickets that they must then sell or give away.

performing rights organization: organization that collects and distributes to its member songwriters and publishers the money to which they are legally entitled when one of their songs is performed, either over the airwaves or in a live performance. There are three in the U.S.: ASCAP, BMI and SESAC.

personal managers: represent artists in numerous ways and help them develop their careers. Typical tasks: negotiating contracts, hiring and dismissing other employees of the artist, reviewing possible material, screening offers, consulting with prospective employers and helping with artist promotions.

pitch: to attempt to sell a song by audition.

play publisher: a publisher of theatrical materials who markets scripts for production by schools, community theaters and other amateur arenas. Works as an agent for a finished play or musical in small producing venues.

press kit: see *submission package.*

print music publisher: company that prints sheet music.

producer: professional employed by a record company or artist/writer who supervises every aspect of recording a song or album.

quavers: the "flags" at the end of the stems of eighth, sixteenth and notes of smaller time value. The quavers should be on the right side of the stem, whether it is pointed up or down.

query letter: a letter asking a producer, manager, etc., to consider one's work. Samples of one's work are usually sent after the receiver responds to the query letter.

query reply card: a stamped postcard enclosed in the envelope with the query letter for easy response from the reciever.

rate: the percentage of royalty as specified by contract.

reply card: see *query reply card* or *submission reply card.*

royalty: percentage of money earned from the sale of records or use of a song.

screening: process by which photographs are made ready for mass duplication through the creation of a dot image. This process is often used for art and type on the J-card.

SESAC: a performing rights organization, originally stood for Society of European Stage Artists and Composers. The smallest of the three performing rights organizations. SESAC screens sample songs before accepting new members. No membership fee.

shell-on printing: process of printing song titles and other information of the cassette shell that involves a mechanical plate and a stamping mechanism.

song shark: one who charges songwriters for services that most reputable companies offer at no cost. For example, a song shark may ask for money in return for a recording contract.

stamp: see *logo.*

stat house: company that sets type and screens photographs.

submission package: a package submitted to prospective managers, producers, agents, etc., which usually includes a photograph, a demo tape, a bio and sometimes a videotape.

submission reply card: a stamped postcard enclosed with the press kit to encourage a response from the receiver.

synopsis: a short summary of a musical script that includes the basic story line and the song titles as they are sung, broken into acts.

track: the separate recordings that can be put together to create a finished tape. Tapes can consist of any number of tracks from two to forty-eight or more, depending on how advanced the studio is. The multiple tracks are eventually mixed down to two—the left and right channels of a radio two-track.

typesetter: professional who sets type and sometimes screens photographs, often hired to help with production of the J-card.

traditional musical: a musical production with form, theme and musical style that are not unusual or progressive.

unsolicited: material sent to a record company, agent, theater, etc., that was not requested and is not expected.

veloxes: high-quality prints (of a logo, picture, etc.) on shiny, sturdy paper, which can be pasted up on other materials and easily copied.

wing space: the offstage area surrounding the playing stage, unseen by the audience, where sets and props are hidden, actors wait for cues, and stagehands prepare to change sets.

INDEX

More Great Books to Help You Sell Your Songs

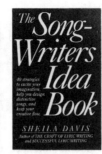

Networking in the Music Business — Who you know can either make (or break) your music career. Discover how to make and capitalize on the contacts you need to succeed.
#10365/$17.95/128 pages/paperback

Beginning Songwriter's Answer Book — This newly revised and updated resource answers the questions most asked by beginning songwriters and gives you the know-how to get started in the music business.
#10376/$16.95/128 pages/paperback

Songwriter's Idea Book — You'll find 40 proven songwriting strategies sure to spark your creativity in this innovative handbook. Plus, learn how to use your unique personality to develop a song writing style.
#10320/$17.95/240 pages

The Craft of Lyric Writing — You'll get a complete guide on writing words for and to music, choosing song formats, and how to write lyrics with universal appeal from bestselling author and songwriter, Sheila Davis.
#10015/$19.95/292 pages/paperback

Making Money in the Music Business — Cash-in on scores of ways to make a profitable living with your musical talent (no matter where you live). This guide covers performing as a solo or in a group, writing music for the radio, jingles and more!
#10174/$18.95/208 pages/paperback

1994 Songwriter's Market — Find the inside tips on how and where to place your songs in more than 2,000 up-to-date listings of song markets. Each listing includes submission requirements and tips from the buyer. Plus

get helpful articles on the ins and outs of the music business.
#10342/$19.95/528 pages

Successful Lyric Writing — Write the kinds of lyrics that dazzle music executives with this hands-on course in writing. Dozens of exercises and demonstrations let you put what you've learned into practice! *#10015/$19.95/ 292 pages/paperback*

Songwriters on Songwriting — You'll share in the triumphs, disappointments, and success secrets of 32 of the world's greatest songwriters as they candidly discuss their art.
#10219/$17.95/196 pages/paperback

The Songwriter's Workshop — With this tape and book workshop, you'll discover how to write lyrics, make a demo, understand MIDI, pitch songs, and more! Plus get loads of inspiration and creativity sparkers.
#10220/$24.95/86 pages plus 2 cassettes

Music Publishing: A Songwriter's Guide — Get a handle on your songwriting career! This practical guide gives you advice you need on types of royalties, subpublishing, songwriter options in publishing and more!
#10195/$18.95/144 pages/paperback